First World War
and Army of Occupation
War Diary
France, Belgium and Germany

37 DIVISION
112 Infantry Brigade
Royal Fusiliers (City of London Regiment)
13th Battalion
1 February 1918 - 31 March 1919

WO95/2538/3

The Naval & Military Press Ltd
www.nmarchive.com
Published in association with The National Archives

Published by

The Naval & Military Press Ltd

Unit 10 Ridgewood Industrial Park,

Uckfield, East Sussex,

TN22 5QE England

Tel: +44 (0) 1825 749494

www.naval-military-press.com

www.nmarchive.com

This diary has been reprinted in facsimile from the original. Any imperfections are inevitably reproduced and the quality may fall short of modern type and cartographic standards.

Contents

Document type	Place/Title	Date From	Date To
Heading	WO95/2538/3		
Heading	13th Bn Roy. Fusiliers Feb 1918-Feb 1919		
War Diary	Campagne	01/02/1918	15/02/1918
War Diary	Cameron Court Glencorse Wood 28 J.14.68.65	16/02/1918	21/02/1918
War Diary	Stirling Castle Sheet 28 J 19 L 9	22/02/1918	28/02/1918
War Diary	Mai Da Camp Sheet 28 If.30C.	01/03/1918	03/03/1918
War Diary	Tower Hamlets Ridge Bn HQ. Sheet 28 J 20 b. 4.4	04/03/1918	10/03/1918
War Diary	Stirling Castle J.19 L. (Sheet 28)	11/03/1918	16/03/1918
War Diary	Maida Camp H. 30 c 2.9 (Sheet 28)	17/03/1918	25/03/1918
War Diary	Manawato Camp Sheet 28 I. 15.C.	26/03/1918	27/03/1918
War Diary	Borre (Hazebrouck 5a 1/100,000)	28/03/1918	28/03/1918
War Diary	Toutencourt	29/03/1918	29/03/1918
War Diary	Rossignol Farm	30/03/1918	31/03/1918
Heading	13th Battn. The Royal Fusiliers. April 1918		
War Diary	Bucquoy Sheet 57 D.N.E. 1/20,000	01/04/1918	05/04/1918
War Diary	Bucquoy	05/04/1918	11/04/1918
War Diary	Gommecourt Sheet 57 D.N.E 1/20,000	12/04/1918	15/04/1918
War Diary	Bois De Warnimont	16/04/1918	24/04/1918
War Diary	E. 23, 24 30 (Sheet 57D. 1/20,000)	25/04/1918	30/04/1918
Miscellaneous	Appendices 47A 48 49 50 50A 51 52 52A 53 54 55		
Map	App 47		
Operation(al) Order(s)	Order No. 171 App 48	01/04/1918	01/04/1918
Miscellaneous	Royal Fusiliers. Order No. 172 App 49	04/04/1918	04/04/1918
Miscellaneous	Nos. 1, 2, 3 & 4 Coys. App 50	04/04/1918	04/04/1918
Miscellaneous	Short Summary Of Operations At Bucquoy On 5/4/16 App 50A	05/04/1918	05/04/1918
Map			
Operation(al) Order(s)	Royal Fusiliers. Order No. 173 App 51	09/04/1918	09/04/1918
Operation(al) Order(s)	13th Bn. Royal Fusiliers. Order No 174 App 52	12/04/1918	12/04/1918
Map	App 52A		
Operation(al) Order(s)	13th Bn. Royal Fusiliers. Order No. 175 App 53	15/04/1918	15/04/1918
Operation(al) Order(s)	13th Bn. Royal Fusiliers. Order No. 176 App 54		
Operation(al) Order(s)	13th Bn. Royal Fusiliers. Order No. 177 App 55	30/04/1918	30/04/1918
Heading	War Diary Of 13th Royal Fusiliers From 1st May 1918 to 31st May 1918 (Volume 34)		
War Diary		01/05/1918	17/05/1918
War Diary	Louvencourt (Sheet 57D I. 34)	18/05/1918	25/05/1918
War Diary	Vauchelles	26/05/1918	31/05/1918
Heading	War Diary Of 13th Bn. Royal Fusiliers. From 1st June 1918 to 30th June 1918 Volume 35		
War Diary	Vauchelles (Sheet 57D 1/40,000 I)	01/06/1918	05/06/1918
War Diary	Bougainville (Sheet 62.E. 1/40,000 O 21)	06/06/1918	10/06/1918
War Diary	Le Bosquel (Sheet 66F 1/40,000 K.28)	11/06/1918	13/06/1918
War Diary	Hebecourt (Sheet 66F 1/40,000 F2)	14/06/1918	20/06/1918
War Diary	Namps-Au-Mont	21/06/1918	21/06/1918
War Diary	Authieule 57.D.	22/06/1918	25/06/1918
War Diary	Souastre	26/06/1918	30/06/1918
Heading	War Diary Of 13th Battn Royal Fusiliers For July 1918 Volume 36		
War Diary	Souastre	01/07/1918	10/07/1918

War Diary	Bocquoy	11/07/1918	13/07/1918
War Diary	Souastre	14/07/1918	19/07/1918
War Diary	Top Trench F.21.d.a.6	20/07/1918	23/07/1918
War Diary	F.19.a. 4.8 Sheet 57D.N.E	24/07/1918	28/07/1918
War Diary	F.21.C. 45.70	29/07/1918	31/07/1918
Heading	War Diary Of 13th R Fusiliers. For Month Of August 1918 Volume XXXVI		
War Diary	N of Bucquoy Ref Sheet 57D. N.E	01/08/1918	01/08/1918
War Diary	Z Area E 23	02/08/1918	04/08/1918
War Diary	Souastre	05/08/1918	09/08/1918
War Diary	Pigeon Wood E 30 4 E 24 d	10/08/1918	11/08/1918
War Diary	Pigeon Wood	12/08/1918	15/08/1918
War Diary	S W of Bucquoy	16/08/1918	21/08/1918
War Diary	W of Bucquoy	22/08/1918	22/08/1918
War Diary	N of Achiet-Le-Pent Sheet 57C.NW.	23/08/1918	23/08/1918
War Diary	SE of Achiet-Le-Grand	23/08/1918	24/08/1918
War Diary	E of Bihucourt	24/08/1918	31/08/1918
Miscellaneous	13th Bn. The Royal Fusiliers. App 84	23/08/1918	23/08/1918
Operation(al) Order(s)	13th Battalion Royal Fusiliers. Order No. 204 App 85	24/08/1918	24/08/1918
War Diary	Sheet. 57C Bihucourt	01/09/1918	03/09/1918
War Diary	Favreuil	03/09/1918	03/09/1918
War Diary	E. of Velu & S of Hermies	04/09/1918	04/09/1918
War Diary	S Of Hermies	04/09/1918	06/09/1918
War Diary	E of Velu	07/09/1918	08/09/1918
War Diary	Beugny	09/09/1918	10/09/1918
War Diary	E. of Velu	11/09/1918	13/09/1918
War Diary	Bilhem	14/09/1918	18/09/1918
War Diary	Bertincourt	19/09/1918	20/09/1918
War Diary	Warlencourt Eaucourt	21/09/1918	29/09/1918
War Diary	E. Of Gouzeaucourt	30/09/1918	30/09/1918
Heading	War Diary Of 13th Bn. Royal Fusiliers For Month Of October 1918 Volume XXXVIII		
War Diary	N. Of Gonnelieu	01/10/1918	01/10/1918
War Diary	N. of Gouzeaucourt	02/10/1918	05/10/1918
War Diary	N.W. of Banteux	06/10/1918	07/10/1918
War Diary	S. Of Lesdain	08/10/1918	10/10/1918
War Diary	Bethencourt	11/10/1918	11/10/1918
War Diary	Caudry	12/10/1918	22/10/1918
War Diary	Caudry Beaurain S. of Briastre S.W. of Beaurain	23/10/1918	24/10/1918
War Diary	Ghissignies	25/10/1918	25/10/1918
War Diary	Salesches	26/10/1918	27/10/1918
War Diary	Neuville	28/10/1918	28/10/1918
War Diary	Beaurain	29/10/1918	31/10/1918
War Diary	Summary Of Operations Carried Out by 13th Bn. Royal Fusiliers 7th to 11th October 1918 App 10		
Operation(al) Order(s)	13th Bn. Royal Fusiliers Order No. 221 App 10	27/10/1918	27/10/1918
Miscellaneous	13th Bn. Royal Fusiliers. Operations 23rd-25th October, 1918		
Miscellaneous	13th Bn. Royal Fusiliers Notes On the attacks.	24/10/1918	24/10/1918
Heading	War Diary Of 13th Bn. Royal Fusiliers For Month Of November 1918 Volume 39		
War Diary	Beaurain	01/11/1918	03/11/1918
War Diary	Salesches	03/11/1918	03/11/1918
War Diary	Ghissignies Fme. De. L'Hopital	04/11/1918	04/11/1918
War Diary	Jolimetz Rond Quesne	04/11/1918	04/11/1918
War Diary	Rond Quesne	05/04/1918	05/04/1918

War Diary	Louvignies	06/11/1918	10/11/1918
War Diary	Bethencourt	11/11/1918	30/11/1918
Miscellaneous	Notes On The Operations 4th 5th November 1918	08/11/1918	08/11/1918
Operation(al) Order(s)	13th Bn. Royal Fusiliers. Order No. 225 App 109	10/11/1918	10/11/1918
Operation(al) Order(s)	13th Bn. Royal Fusiliers. Order No. 225 App 110	30/11/1918	30/11/1918
Map			
Heading	War Diary Of 13th Battn. Royal Fusiliers For The Month Of December 1918 Volume 40		
War Diary	Bethencourt	01/12/1918	01/12/1918
War Diary	Bermerain	02/12/1918	02/12/1918
War Diary	Wargnies Le-Grand	03/12/1918	14/12/1918
War Diary	Bellignies	15/12/1918	15/12/1918
War Diary	La Longueville	16/12/1918	18/12/1918
War Diary	Binche	19/12/1918	19/12/1918
War Diary	Souvret	20/12/1918	20/12/1918
War Diary	Ransart	21/12/1918	31/12/1918
Heading	13th Bn Ryl Fusiliers War Diary Volume XLIII January 1919		
Miscellaneous	13th S. Battalion Royal Fusiliers App 118		
War Diary	Ransart (Namur. 8 I.F.)	01/01/1919	31/01/1919
Heading	War Diary Of 13th Bn The Ryl Fusiliers For The Month Of February 1919 Volume 45		
War Diary	Ransart (Namur 8. I.F.)	03/02/1919	27/02/1919
War Diary	Ransart Ref. Map Namur 8	01/03/1919	31/03/1919
Miscellaneous	Effective Strength For February 1st 1919		
Miscellaneous	Translation Of a letter from the Maire Of Caudry.		
Miscellaneous			
Miscellaneous	Legend		

37TH DIVISION
112TH INFY BDE

13TH BN ROY. FUSILIERS

FEB 1918-FEB 1919

FROM 111 BDE 37 DIV

Army Form C. 2118.

112/37

WAR DIARY
or
INTELLIGENCE SUMMARY.
(Erase heading not required.)

13 R F

Vol 29

Instructions regarding War Diaries and Intelligence Summaries are contained in F. S. Regs., Part II. and the Staff Manual respectively. Title pages will be prepared in manuscript.

Place	Date	Hour	Summary of Events and Information	Remarks and references to Appendices
Cantaing [illegible]	1/2/18		Training. Platoon Competition for best Platoon in turn out, marching & drill [illegible] held. Judged by G.O.C. 111 Inf Bde. No 4 Coy Platoon under 2nd Lt [illegible] [illegible] R.C. won. [illegible] Competition [illegible] won by No 4 Coy. Temp Capt C. Pratt M.C. appointed 2 in Command [illegible]	Feb '18 – Feb '19
	4/2/18		Training. Brigade Sports held. Capt P.M. Stewart, 2/Lts F.L. Kirman, J. Davis, A/J Rowland joined Bn.	
	[illegible]/2/18		Day passed quietly in [illegible]	
	[illegible]/2/18		Under the new organisation, the 13 R. Fus. were transferred from the 111 Inf Bde to the 112 Inf Bde – a much regretted parting. The 111 Inf Bde [illegible] Bde moved into the forward area leaving the Bn [illegible]. The remaining Bns of 112 Inf Bde [illegible] 112 Inf Bde [illegible] now formed. 6 Bedf R & [illegible] R. [illegible] Bde training [illegible]. Lt Col R.A. Smith went on leave. Command taken over by Major C. Pratt M.C.	28 P. (15 sheets)

A7092). Wt. W12839/M1293 750,000. 1/17. D. D & L., Ltd. Forms/C2118/14.

Instructions regarding War Diaries and Intelligence Summaries are contained in F. S. Regs., Part II. and the Staff Manual respectively. Title pages will be prepared in manuscript.

WAR DIARY
or
INTELLIGENCE SUMMARY.
(*Erase heading not required.*)

Army Form C. 2118.

Place	Date	Hour	Summary of Events and Information	Remarks and references to Appendices
CAMPAGNE	5/2/18		Training continued	
	6/2/18		Training continued. Batt marched to St OMER	
	7/2/18.		Batt inspected by G.O.C 112 Inf Bde	
	8/2/18		Training continued. Message of congratulation received from G.O.C 112 Inf Bde on	
			excellent turn out of Batt & transport	
	9/2/18		Draft of 8 officers & 213 O.R. from disbanded 20 R Fus joined Batt. Officers	
			T/Capt G.G. Ziegler T/2Lt (A/Capt) F.W. Browne Lieut B.E.G. Marshall T/2Lieut A.E. Floyd	
			C.E. Vickers M.M. 2/Lt D.C.Z. A.H. Taylor & R.H. Worley	
	10/2/18		Training continued	
	11/2/18		Training continued	
	12/2/18		Training continued	
	13/2/18		Training continued. Move order for Transport to start for forward area issued	App 30
	14/2/18		Transport moved to ST PIERREBROUCK	

D. D. & L., London, E.C. (A7883) Wt. W807/M1672 350,000 4/17 Sch. 52a Forms C/2118/14

Instructions regarding War Diaries and Intelligence Summaries are contained in F. S. Regs., Part II. and the Staff Manual respectively. Title pages will be prepared in manuscript.

WAR DIARY
or
INTELLIGENCE SUMMARY.
(Erase heading not required.)

Army Form C. 2118.

Place	Date	Hour	Summary of Events and Information	Remarks and references to Appendices
CAMPAGNE	14/2/18		Battn Transport moved to STRAZEELE — Order No 156 [illegible]	App 31
			Capt P.A. STEWART & 2 Lieut F.R. SLINGERLAND left Battalion to proceed to England	
			2 Lieut C.S. JONES joined Batt.	
	15/2/18		Batt moved to FORRESTER CAMP (28 H30 d 6 5) via EBBLINGHEM [illegible] (by train) – FORRESTER CAMP (by march route) — Transport moved from STRAZEELE to CAFE BELGE.	
GLENCORSE WOOD 28 J14 a 65 55	16/2/18		Order No 157 issued. Batt [illegible] CAMERON [illegible] for 12 R.B. (20 Div) Relief completed without incident 8.15 PM. No [illegible] Coy [illegible] posts, No 1 Coy left posts, No 2 in Support, No 4 in Reserve. Batt HQ in GLENCORSE WOOD (J 14 a 60.55). Dispositions as shown on attached map	App 32 App 33
	17/2/18		Day passed quietly. Slight shelling No 6 post. Patrols visited banks of [illegible] to J 7 a 0 3 (?) [illegible] to J16 b 4.0. No enemy [illegible] met. Ground very difficult owing to [illegible] Warning [illegible] enemy [illegible] artillery [illegible] to [illegible] Following officers joined Batt T/2 Lt H A Pye, A B Blaxam, E R J Bowler.	

D. D. & L., London, E.C. (A7883) Wt. W593/M1672 350,000 4/17 Sch. 52a Forms/C/2118/14

Instructions regarding War Diaries and Intelligence Summaries are contained in F. S. Regs., Part II. and the Staff Manual respectively. Title pages will be prepared in manuscript.

WAR DIARY
or
INTELLIGENCE SUMMARY.
(Erase heading not required.)

Army Form C. 2118.

Place	Date	Hour	Summary of Events and Information	Remarks and references to Appendices
	18/2/18		Patrols reconnoitred POLYGON BEEK as far as junction with REUTELBEEK. No enemy were met. Patrol also examined REUTELBEEK without meeting any enemy.	
	[illegible]/2/18		Day passed quietly.	
	19/2/18?		Day passed quietly. Patrols again searched triangle of REUTELBEEK – POLYGON BEEK – front line. No signs of enemy. Track was [illegible] & Bed R. [illegible]	
	20/2/18?		Day passed quietly. Orders were received to attempt to [illegible] a presence [not been located] during or after [illegible] to be carried out by 1st OTAGO Bn on left. It was however found impossible owing to our own machine gun programme on J.16d & J.17c	
	21/2/18	3.30am	1st Otago Bn [illegible] posts about J.17a 75.75 [illegible] enemy barrage on posts & front line.	
			Order No 158 issued. [2 Coy] 1/10 R.Fus [+2 Coy 13 R.B.] to relieve 13 R.Fus. who were to go into support behind 1st Essex R. holding [illegible] Road sector. The destination of two companies only was given by Brigade & it was not until the relief of the support & reserve companies was very nearly complete that message was received from ~~Staff Captain~~ Brigade Major reading ~~[illegible]~~ "Two companies of your Battalion will be accommodated in JACKDAW TUNNELS area. If you have been unable to find accommodation for remainder they can go to [illegible] BURGOMASTER CAMP." No 214 [illegible]	App. 34.

D. D. & L., London, E.C. (A7883) Wt. W603/M1672 350,000 4/17 Sch. 52a Forms C/21/8/14

Instructions regarding War Diaries and Intelligence Summaries are contained in F. S. Regs., Part II. and the Staff Manual respectively. Title pages will be prepared in manuscript.

WAR DIARY
or
INTELLIGENCE SUMMARY.
(Erase heading not required.)

Army Form C. 2118.

Place	Date	Hour	Summary of Events and Information	Remarks and references to Appendices
			marched to BURGOMASTER CAMP (H 34 a 4.7) DICKEBUSCH. No 1 & 3 Coys moved into	
			JACKDAW TUNNELS (J 19 a 4.9). B.H HQ to STIRLING CASTLE (J 19 b 30 85) Relief	
			Relief complete at 10 PM.	
			Lt Col R G SMITH MC returned from leave & took over command of Bn	
			Visits to HQ of front line Bn. reconnaissance during night	
STIRLING CASTLE Sheet 28 J 19 a 4.9	22/2/18		Working parties on forward area found [crossed out] Route tracks & trenches	
			reconnaissance. Order No 159. issued. No 2 Coy relieved No 3 Coy in JACKDAW	App 35
			TUNNELS. No 3 Coy proceeded on relief to BURGOMASTER CAMP. No 4 Coy moved	
			into new infantry tunnels STIRLING TUNNELS No 1. J 13 d 67 20.	
			Defence Scheme (provisional) issued. 7/9th W S Fus joined from 20 Bde.	App 36
	23/2/18		Bn on working parties	
	24/2/18		B.H. on working parties.	
	25/2/18		B.H on working parties. It was informed from Brigade that STIRLING TUNNELS 2	
			were ready for occupation. No 3 company was ordered up from DICKEBUSCH	
			in consequence. It was found on investigation that the tunnels were not	
			ready. & on arrival at JACKDAW TUNNELS the company had to be sent back.	

D. D. & L., London, E.C. (A7883) Wt. W807/M1672 350,000 4/17 Sch. 52a. Forms C/2118/14

Instructions regarding War Diaries and Intelligence Summaries are contained in F. S. Regs., Part II. and the Staff Manual respectively. Title pages will be prepared in manuscript.

WAR DIARY
or
INTELLIGENCE SUMMARY.
(*Erase heading not required.*)

Army Form C. 2118.

Place	Date	Hour	Summary of Events and Information	Remarks and references to Appendices
	25/2/18	11.50PM	Enemy opened a heavy bombardment with gas shell on area J13 c & d J14 c J19 a & b & J20 a. It is probable that about 5 batteries were shooting. Rate of fire about 4 rounds per gun per minute – gas shell with about 1 per cent of H.E. About 2000 rounds were fired. From examination of ground it appears to be a practice shoot on tracks [illegible] & routes by which our forward troops to TOWER HAMLETS would come. Shelling died down at about 12.20 AM & except for short bursts, was confined to the high ground in J19 & J25.	
			7 O.R. HQ runners were gassed. 2Lt R.A. BARKER joined Bn from 20 R.F.	
	26/2/18		Order No 160 issued. Bn on working parties. 1st Essex Regt relieved Bn in support. Bn withdrawn into Reserve at MAIDA CAMP H 30 a 0 2. Relief completed 9.35 PM without incident.	App 37
	27/2/18		A prisoner of the 8th R.I.R. (18 Res Div) was captured near POLDERHOEK CHATEAU. He stated that the enemy was about to attack to regain the ridge & probably would do so on morning of 28th. Consequently the reserve Bn of 112 Bde 13 R.F. was put under orders of the Bde to be in state of readiness from 6 PM. Order No 161 issued.	App 38

Instructions regarding War Diaries and Intelligence Summaries are contained in F. S. Regs., Part II. and the Staff Manual respectively. Title pages will be prepared in manuscript.

Army Form C. 2118.

WAR DIARY
or
INTELLIGENCE SUMMARY.
(*Erase heading not required.*)

Place	Date	Hour	Summary of Events and Information	Remarks and references to Appendices
	27/2/18		2Lts B ARMSTRONG + E BUTTERWORTH joined Batt	
	28/2/18		Batt standing by waiting to move.	
			2Lt T.F. OXTON joined Battalion.	

[illegible signature]
B[illegible]

D. D. & L., London, E.C. (A7883) Wt. W803/M1672 350,000 4/17 Sch. 52a. Forms C/2118/14

Instructions regarding War Diaries and Intelligence Summaries are contained in F. S. Regs., Part II. and the Staff Manual respectively. Title pages will be prepared in manuscript.

WAR DIARY
or
INTELLIGENCE SUMMARY.
(Erase heading not required.)

Army Form C. 2118.

13 Royal Fus

Vol 30

Place	Date	Hour	Summary of Events and Information	Remarks and references to Appendices
MAIDA CAMP Sheet 28 H.30c.	1.3.18		Battalion still standing by in state of readiness. Ordinary training carried out.	
			2nd Lieut. M.V. Vaughan, M.C. left Battn. for 6 month's tour of duty in England & is struck off strength.	
			Strength 1/3/18 - 58 Officers & 849 O.R.	
	2.3.18		Cold & snow. Wind N.W. strong. Battn. still standing to. Night passed fairly quietly.	
	3.3.18		Without incident.	
TOWER HAMLETS RIDGE. Bn. Hq. Sheet 28 J.20b.4.4	4.3.18		Order No. 162 issued. Battn. moved into trenches astride MENIN ROAD. Night dark & rainy. No moon. Owing to bad guides relief of 6th Beds. Regt. was not complete until 11.40 p.m. Night passed fairly quietly. ~~Disposition map attached.~~	App 38. App 39.
	5.3.18	5.20am	Private soldier of 31st R.I.R. (18th Res. Div.) was taken prisoner by No 2 Coy. On interrogation he appeared to know of no offensive action to be undertaken against this front, but had heard that 18th Res. Div. was to be relieved about beginning of April to take part in an offensive further South.	
			Enemy's artillery fairly active, chiefly about PERTH AVENUE & Right Coy. H.Q. J.21.a.4.0.	
			Capt. R.G. Vanneck, M.C. left Battalion for 6 month's tour of duty in England & is struck off strength.	
			2nd Lieut. R.K. Keller joined Battalion.	
	6.3.18.	1.5a.m 1.20am	Counter preparation was fired by Group Artillery on whole sector to 1.15 a.m. Enemy retaliation slight.	
			During day enemy artillery very active on J.21.a. & J.20.b.	
			Patrol of 2nd Lieut. H.K.Kernott, DCM.MM. & 4 O.R. ran into strong party of enemy with two light M.Guns about J.21.b.7.3. & were forced to withdraw.	
			Patrol under 2nd Lieut. J.Davis reconnoitred MENIN ROAD as far as crater at J.21.d.60.99 where patrol was fired on.	
			Draft of 95. O.R. joined Batt.	

29.B. (15 sheets)

D. D. & L., London, E.C. (A8001) Wt. W1771/M2031 750,000 5/17 Sch. 52 Forms C2118/14

Instructions regarding War Diaries and Intelligence Summaries are contained in F. S. Regs., Part II. and the Staff Manual respectively. Title pages will be prepared in manuscript.

WAR DIARY
or
INTELLIGENCE SUMMARY.

(Erase heading not required.)

Army Form C. 2118.

Place	Date	Hour	Summary of Events and Information	Remarks and references to Appendices
	7.3.18.	5 a.m.	15 minutes counter preparation was fired by covering artillery. Enemy did not reply. During day hostile artillery below normal. Inter-company reliefs were carried out at dusk. No 3 Coy. relieving No 4 Coy. N. of MENIN ROAD & No 1 Coy. relieving No 2 Coy. on S. side. No 2 Coy. moved into support. No 4 Coy. into Reserve.	
	8.3.18.	1 a.m.	Message received from Brigade that enemy intend to attack during night to capture high ground N.W. of GHELUVELT. Companies warned & prepared. Counter preparation fired at Dawn without reply.	
	8.3.18.	6.30 a.m.	Hostile artillery commenced shelling front & support systems with 77 & 105 mm on both sides MENIN ROAD. The shelling became very much fierce after 9.30 a.m. & continued with a short break between 1.0 & 1.30 p.m. until about 5.0 p.m. Orders were sent to Reserve Coy. to move up at 6.30 p.m. from ZILLEBEKE.	
		5.30 p.m.	Enemy shelling very heavy N. of MENIN ROAD.	
		5.45 p.m.	S.O.S. sent up by Battalion on left. Artillery answered on whole sector within two minutes. No attack developed on Battalion front, but enemy shelling badly damaged No 3 Coy. N. of this road.	
		6.30 p.m.	Following message received from No 3 Coy. "Please send as many stretcher bearers as possible - only few men left to carry on & no officers fit to carry on. 2 officers killed, 2 wounded. Please send reinforcements as soon as possible. A CLARK, Sergt. No 3 Coy. " Platoon of No 2 Coy. garrisoning S.P.5 was sent forward immediately & the platoons of No 4 Coy. in CLAPHAM JUNCTION under 2nd Lieut H.J. Rowlands followed shortly. The latter was	
		8.30 p.m.	able to clear up the situation & reported to Battn. H.Q. that the front line was intact shortly after the arrival of Capt. P.E. Lewis with the remainder of No 4 Coy. Casualties sustained during the day :- Killed - A/Capt. F.W. Bower, 2nd Lieut. W. Henderson & 7 O.R. Wounded - Capt. T.H. Whitehead, M.C. Lieut. B.E.A.Marshall, 2nd Lieut. M.N.Wilcock, 2nd Lieut. A.B. Blain (at duty) 2nd Lieut. F.L. Kilham &33 O.R. During the evening, information was received that the enemy had succeeded in entering the trenches of the Battn. on the left, 13th K.R.R.C. but that they were being bombed out by the 10th R.Fus. 2 platoons 6th Bedford Regt. reinforced S.P.6 during the night. Night passed quietly.	

D. D. & L., London, E.C.
(A8001) Wt. W1771/M2031 750,000 5/17 Sch. 52 Forms/C2118/14

Army Form C. 2118.

Instructions regarding War Diaries and Intelligence Summaries are contained in F. S. Regs., Part II. and the Staff Manual respectively. Title pages will be prepared in manuscript.

WAR DIARY
or
INTELLIGENCE SUMMARY.
(Erase heading not required.)

Place	Date	Hour	Summary of Events and Information	Remarks and references to Appendices
	9.3.18.		30 men of new draft moved up to replace 2 platoons 6th Beds. Regt. Weather very misty. Artillery activity below normal.	
	10.3.18.		Weather misty - cold - fine. Artillery activity normal. Order No. 163 issued. 1st Essex Regt. relieved Battalion. Relief complete 11.40 p.m. Battn. withdrawn into Support. 2 Coys. in JACKDAW TUNNELS - 2 Coys. in STIRLING TUNNELS. Battn. H.Q. - STIRLING CASTLE.	App 40.
STIRLING CASTLE J.19b. (Sheet 28)	11.3.18		Working parties. Weather fine & misty.	
	12.3.18.		Night working parties. Weather fine.	
	13.3.18		Night working parties.	
	14.3.18		Working parties. Battn. in line (1st Essex Regt.) raided enemy. Enemy barrage light. Order No 164 issued.	App 41.
	15.3.18.	4.15 a.m.	Enemy opened heavy bombardment on TOWER HAMLETS RIDGE which continued until 5.0 a.m. Working parties continued.	
	16.3.18.		Working parties. 1st Essex Regt. relieved Battn. in Support Line. Battalion withdrawn into Reserve at MAIDA CAMP (H.30.c.2.9.) No 1 Coy. was slightly shelled on moving out near ZILLEBEKE.	
MAIDA CAMP. H.30 c 2.9 (Sheet 28)	17.3.18.		Bathing & clearing up. Lt-Col. R.A.Smith, M.C. went on course to Army Gas School. Major C. Pratt, M.C. took over Command.	

D. D. & L., London, E.C. (A8004) Wt. W1771/M2031 750,000 5/17 Sch. 52 Forms/C2118/14

Instructions regarding War Diaries and Intelligence Summaries are contained in F. S. Regs., Part II. and the Staff Manual respectively. Title pages will be prepared in manuscript.

WAR DIARY
or
INTELLIGENCE SUMMARY.
(Erase heading not required.)

Army Form C. 2118.

Place	Date	Hour	Summary of Events and Information	Remarks and references to Appendices
	18/3/18		No. 7547 Sgt. A. Clark, No 3 Coy. awarded M.M. by G.O.C. XXII Corps for gallantry & devotion to duty E. of YPRES on 8/3/18. After all his officers had been either killed or wounded by enemy bombardment, this N.C.O. took command of & redisposed the remaining men of his company under heavy shell & trench mortar fire, until such time as reinforcements could be sent, thereby denying to the enemy an attempted lodgment in our front line posts.	
	19/3/18		Without incident. Enemy long range guns shelling DICKEBUSCH & vicinity. 2nd Lieut. F.L. Kilham transferred to England & struck off strength.	
	20/3/18		Without incident.	
	21/3/18		Order No. 165 issued.	App. 42.
	22/3/18		Battn. moved into trenches on MENIN ROAD relieving 6th Bedford Regt. Relief passed without incident. Weather very clear.	
	23/3/18		Day passed quietly. 2 O.R. killed - 3 wounded by T.M. fire.	
	24/3/18		Day passed quietly. Inter-company relief took place.	
	25/3/18		Battn. relieved by 13th R.Bde. & moved into reserve at MANAWATU CAMP. 2nd Lieut. F.B. Radford killed in action. Buried at J.20.b.4.4.	
MANAWATU CAMP SHEET 28. I.15.C	26/3/18		Battn. bathed & cleaning up.	
		10 P.M	Verbal orders from Brigade to commence storing surplus stores at ABEELE forthwith. Storgage commenced.	
	27/3/18	1. A.M.	Brigade wired that Battn. would move to STAPLE to-day. Order No. 166 issued.	App 43.

D. D. & L., London, E.C.
(A8001) Wt. W1771/M2031 750,000 5/17 Sch. 52 Forms/C2118/14

Army Form C. 2118.

WAR DIARY
or
INTELLIGENCE SUMMARY.

(Erase heading not required.)

Instructions regarding War Diaries and Intelligence Summaries are contained in F. S. Regs., Part II. and the Staff Manual respectively. Title pages will be prepared in manuscript.

Place	Date	Hour	Summary of Events and Information	Remarks and references to Appendices
BORRE (HAZEBROUCK 5a 1/100,000)		11.30A.M	Battn. embussed on YPRES - KRUISSTRAATHOEK Road. Arrived CAESTRE area. Battn. billeted by 5.30 p.m. H.Q. in BORRE. Companies in billets - very widely spread. Draft of 43 O.R. joined Battn.	
	28/3/18	5.30A.M	Orders received No 4 Coy. to go in advance. Orders 167 & 168 issued.	app. 44 + 45.
	29/3/18	7.30AM	Battn. detrained at MONDICOURT & marched to TOUTENCOURT.	
TOUTENCOURT		4.0 P.M.	Arrival at TOUTENCOURT. Battn. in billets by 4.30 p.m. Warning order received to be ready to move at 10.0 a.m. 30/3/18 to COUIN area.	
	30/3/18	7.0A.M.	Orders received to move to COUIN area. Order No. 169 issued. Division transferred to IV Corps.	app. 46.
ROSSIGNOL FARM.		4.0 P.M.	Battn. settled in billets at ROSSIGNOL FARM. Commanding Officer reconnoitred line in BUCQUOY Sector.	
	31/3/18		Order No 170 issued. Relief passed without incident. Strength 31/3/18 - 52 Officers & 1022 O.R.	app. 47.

[signature] 2nd Lieut. & Asst. Adjt.
for Lt-Col. Commdg. 13th Bn. ROYAL FUSILIERS.

D. D. & L., London, E.C.
(A8001) Wt. W1771/M2031 750,000 5/17 Sch. 52 Forms/C2118/14

112th Inf.Bde.
37th Div.

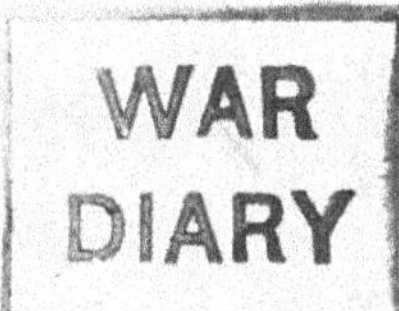

13th BATTN. THE ROYAL FUSILIERS.

A P R I L

1 9 1 8

Attached:

Appendices 47A to 55.

Instructions regarding War Diaries and Intelligence Summaries are contained in F. S. Regs., Part II. and the Staff Manual respectively. Title pages will be prepared in manuscript.

WAR DIARY
or
INTELLIGENCE SUMMARY.
(Erase heading not required.)

Army Form C. 2118.

13 RF Vol 31

Place	Date	Hour	Summary of Events and Information	Remarks and references to Appendices
BUCQUOY SHEET 57 D.N.E. 20,000	April 1st		Battn. in line. (disposition map attached) STRENGTH. 52 Off + 1023 O.R.	App 47A
		7.15 AM	Enemy attempted to rush bombing posts held by No 2 Coy. at L.10.a.35.40 & L.10.a.40.50 & were repulsed. A second attempt was made in the Southern part shortly afterwards, which was also dealt with. 2nd Lieut. J. Davis displayed great gallantry, after being wounded he continued to direct bombers, standing on the top of the parapet. Casualties :- 2 Officers (2nd Lieut. J. Davis - Lieut. N.C. Hinton, wounded, 12 O.R. 4.5 Howitzers fired on enemy & effectually cleared their trench.	
		12 MN	Enemy registered front line in L.3.c.4.0. L.9.b.8.8. with aeroplane observation. Battalion H.Q. moved to L.3.c.0.8. Order No. 171 issued.	App. 48
	2nd		Day passed quietly. Re-adjustment in line made in accordance with Order No 171.	
	3rd		4 prisoners (126 R.I.R.) were taken on Railway in L.9.a. & also 1 - 2Gd. R.I.R. (1st Gd.Res. Div)	
	4th	1 AM	Patrol of Capt. J.K. Gwinnell & 2 O.R. met 2 enemy (17th Div) about L.9.a.5.1., killing one & took second prisoner. A prisoner of 2Gd R.I.R. was also taken prisoner.	
		4 PM	Enemy bombarded No 1 Coy's line from E & S. very heavily for about an hour. Casualties :- 2nd Lieut. C.F. Bishop (killed) 2nd Lieut. R.A. Barker (Wounded) 2nd Lieut. J.L. Boyle (Wounded, at duty) 1 O.R. killed, 8 wounded. During these four days enemy exposed himself freely & a large number were accounted for by snipers. Order No.172 & J189 issued.	App 49-50
	5th	5.30 AM	Enemy opened a heavy bombardment from E. & S. on battery positions. This coincided with an attack on ROSSIGNOL WOOD carried out by 63rd Inf. Bde.	
		6.30 AM	Enemy extended bombardment to cover BUCQUOY, L.3.c. & the whole front line trenches On E. & S. of the village, & all communications. Bombardment very severe. No 3 Coys & No. 1 Coys. trench line practically obliterated, but casualties not severe owing to good cover obtainable in deep dug-outs. No 2 Coys. line & No 4 Coys. escaped, the enemy shelling not being so accurate.	
		8.30 AM	No 4 Coy. report enemy likely to attack. Information passed to Battn. & Battn. on left.	
		8.45 AM	The enemy artillery lifted off the front line & spasmodic attacks were begun.	

D. D. & L., London, E.C. (A8004) Wt. W1771/M2031 750,000 5/17 Sch. 52 Forms/C2118/14

30 G. (24 sheets)

Instructions regarding War Diaries and Intelligence Summaries are contained in F. S. Regs., Part II. and the Staff Manual respectively. Title pages will be prepared in manuscript.

WAR DIARY
or
INTELLIGENCE SUMMARY.
(Erase heading not required.)

Army Form C. 2118.

Place	Date	Hour	Summary of Events and Information	Remarks and references to Appendices
BUCQUOY	5th	8.45 A.M	No 4 Coy. easily repulsed enemy in L.8.b. with Lewis Gun & rifle fire. No 2 & No 3 Coy. were subjected to strong bombing attacks at L.10.a.3.3. & L.10.a.3.5. respectively. The latter was easily beaton off, but the enemy succeeded in driving our men back to Coy.H.Q. at L.10.a.0.5. in the Southern attack. An immediate bombing counter-attack undertaken -by 2nd Lieut. H.Kirk,D.C.M. & No. 4674 Sgt. Bowden, H.R. restored the position, the enemy retiring leaving several dead, including an Officer.	
			Nos 1 & 3 Coys. reported line intact & quite happy.	
		10 A.M.	About the same time men of the 1/8th Lancs. Fus. were found retiring on the Western side of BUCQUOY. On enquiry it was found that practically the whole of the 1/8th Lanc. Fus. had retired, with the exception of elements of their Right Company. Lt-Col. R.A. Smith, M.C. at once left Battn. H.Q. & proceeded to 1/8th Lancs.Fus. H.Q. & from thence onwards practically took over the re-organisation of the line by turning back the men of that Battn.	
		10.40 A.M.	Message was at once sent to Nos. 1, 2 & 3 Coys. 'Enemy are reported to be in the village about cross roads L.3.c.90.60. If position is such & Battn. on your left have withdrawn, withdraw through front line & take up position approximately on sunken road L.2.b.9.4. - L.3.c.00.40.'	
		12 noon	No 4 Coy. was ordered to form their support platoon on road between L.2.d.95.25 & cross roads L.3.c.05.85. Battn. H.Q. details were at same time extended Northwards from this point to cover sunken roads & exits from village.	
			No 3 Coy. ascertained that practically the whole of 1/8th Lancs. Fus. had evacuated the position, & that the enemy had occupied the wood in L.3.d. & L.4.c. up to which point they had rushed a T.M. & 2 M.G.	
			No 2 Coy. then commenced their withdrawal by way of sunken road in L.9.b. - L.3.d.	
			No 3 Coy. having destroyed their dug-outs, etc., followed, both retirements covered by No 1 Coys. support platoon under 2nd Lieut. C.E.Vickers, M.M. who got into position along the Southern bank of the sunken road & engaged enemy in L.3.d. The withdrawal of	

D. D. & L., London, E.C. (A8001) Wt. W1771/M2031 750,000 5/17 Sch. 52 Forms/C2118/14

Army Form C. 2118.

Instructions regarding War Diaries and Intelligence Summaries are contained in F. S. Regs., Part II. and the Staff Manual respectively. Title pages will be prepared in manuscript.

WAR DIARY

or

INTELLIGENCE SUMMARY.

(Erase heading not required.)

Place	Date	Hour	Summary of Events and Information	Remarks and references to Appendices
	5th		No 2 Coy. somewhat uncovered the flank of No 1 Coy. who were rushed before they could get clear. Heavy fighting took place around the Coy H.Q. L.9.b.1.8. which had been partially blown in & several men buried, & the company were only able to extricate themselves at the cost of several men of the H.Q. snipers & the Coy. signal station being taken prisoners. The O.C.Coy. A/Capt. J.K. Gwinnell, was also wounded during this period.	
		2.0 P.M.	By 2.0 p.m. the position of Companies was approximately as follows:- No 4 Coy. on right in their original line, with one platoon L.2.d.99.22 - L.3.a.05 along sunken track. The line of sunken track was continued by 2 platoons of No 1 Coy. Battn. H.Q. details & carrying platoon under 2nd Lieut. G.S. Gibbons. North of this line No 2 Coy. were re-organising and taking up a line in the orchards in the N.W. corner of L.2.a. No 3 Coy. & 1 platoon No 1 Coy. occupied trench running from L.2.a.2.2. - L.2.a.6.8. Battn. H.Q. moved its position back to L.2.a.2.2. North of this again, 2nd Lieut. R.K.Keller, 13th R.Fus. (attached 112 T.M.Bty) was holding on to an advanced position about cross roads L.3.a.85.35. with a mixed group of Nos. 1 & 2 Coys. a few of 1/8th Lancs. Fus. & some of 112th T.M.Bty. The enemy showed no signs of pressing home the attack, & the line was quickly re-organised. H.Q. details were relieved by a platoon of No 1 Coy. opposite late Battn. H.Q. & the whole of the 3 platoons No 1 Coy. & the carrying platoon under 2nd Lieut. G.S. Gibbons were placed under command of Capt. L.F. Woodforde.	
		2.15 P.M.	A small counter-attack had been undertaken in the meanwhile by the 1/8th Lancs. Fus. in which the C.O. & 2nd in Command were both killed. At same time the 1/5th Lancs. Fus. were moved up into the gap on the left & about 4.0 p.m. a counter-attack was undertaken by the 1/5th Lancs Fus. Nos. 2 & 1 Coys. were ordered to conform, but were held up by heavy machine gun fire. The 1/5th Lancs. Fus. also made little progress.	
		5 P.M	The sunken road held by a platoon of No 4 Coy. had in the meanwhile become untenable owing to heavy enfilade machine gun fire. No 4 Coys. platoon was therefore withdrawn, & the line adjusted as follows :- L.2.d.27.21 to junction of road & trench L.2.d.40.72. (No 4 Coy) - thence Eastwards a line of posts as far as cross roads L.3.c.05.82.(No 2 Coy) - thence to L.3.a.3.0. (No 1 Coy) -thence N.E. to L.3.a.42.45 (one company 6th Bedford.Reg.) in touch at this point with 1/5th Lancs Fus. No 3 Coy. in support in trench running N. & S. L.2.b. & d.	

D. D. & L., London, E.C.
(A8004) Wt. W1771/M2031 750,000 5/17 Sch. 52 Forms/C2118/14

Instructions regarding War Diaries and Intelligence Summaries are contained in F. S. Regs., Part II. and the Staff Manual respectively. Title pages will be prepared in manuscript.

WAR DIARY
or
INTELLIGENCE SUMMARY.

(Erase heading not required.)

Army Form C. 2118.

Place	Date	Hour	Summary of Events and Information	Remarks and references to Appendices
			Enemy did not resume attack during the night.	App 50A
	6th		Re-organisation carried out ; No 3 Company relieved 'A' Coy. 6th Bedford. Regt. during night 6/7th. One prisoner 2nd Guards Res.Div. was taken by No 4 Coy. in the early morning. Day quiet. Rain. Enemy artillery shelled trench through L.2.b. & d.	
	7th		Day passed quietly. Rain & Wind, clearing towards evening. W.30. & 36 issued. Battalion was relieved by 2/7th W.Yorks Regt. & moved into support in Strong Points in K.30.b.	
	8th	5 A.M.	Enemy shelled position with Blue Cross gas. Otherwise without incident.	
	9th		Order No. 173 issued. 8th Som. L.I. relieved Battn. in E.20.b. Battn. withdrawn to line of old billeting position W of HEBUTERNE in K.2.c.	App 51
	10th 11th	?	Refitting & re-organising. Men bathing at FONQUEVILLERS under enemy shell fire.	
GOMMECOURT SHEET 57D.NE 1/20,000	12th		Battn. relieved 13th R.Bde. in trenches in GOMMECOURT sector. Dispositions as in attached map. Night quiet. Order No. 174 issued.	App 52 App 52A
	13th		Without incident.	
	14th		Without incident.	
	15th		Except for slight hostile artillery activity on right company front - causing a few casualties + enemy very quiet. Two men of 139 I.R. walked into our lines in the fog. One was shot, the other attempted to escape, but was later captured by 10th R.F. on our right. No 2 Company relieved No 1 Coy. No 4 Coy relieved No 3 Coy.	

D. D. & L., London, E.C.
(A8001) Wt. W1771/M2031 750,000 5/17 Sch. 52 Forms/C2118/14

Army Form C. 2118.

*Instructions regarding War Diaries and Intelligence Summaries are contained in F. S. Regs., Part II. and the Staff Manual respectively. Title pages will be prepared in manuscript.

WAR DIARY
or
INTELLIGENCE SUMMARY.

(Erase heading not required.)

Place	Date	Hour	Summary of Events and Information	Remarks and references to Appendices
	16th		Order No. 175 issued. 1/5 Lanc.Fus. relieved Battn. Relief complete 2.a.m. 17th.	App 53
			Battn. moved to camp in BOIS DE WARNIMONT S. of AUTHIE.	
BOIS DE WARNIMONT	17th		Refitting.	
	18th		Training.	
	19th		Training.	
	20th		Working parties on RED LINE.	
	21st.		Battn. practised manning RED LINE.	
	22nd		Training.	
	23rd		Training. Lieut.F.V.Shaw rejoined Battalion.	
	24th		Order No. 176 issued. Battn. relieved 2/4th Duke of Wellingtons in Reserve to BUCQUOY	App 54
			Sector.area : PIGEON WOOD - LA BRAYELLE FARM .	
			Battn. H.Q. in the 'Z' (E.23.c.)	
F.23. 24 + 30. (SHEET 57D. 1/20,000)	25th		Work on PURPLE LINE defences. No 2 Coy. in PIGEON WOOD were heavily shelled during the afternoon.	
	26th		Quiet. Work carried out on defences.	
			Lieut. H.W.Daniel M.C. & 2nd Lieut. A.A.Allen,M.C. rejoined Battn.	

D. D. & L., London, E.C.
(A7853) Wt. W593/M1672 350,000 1/17 Sch. 52a Forms C/2118/14

Instructions regarding War Diaries and Intelligence Summaries are contained in F. S. Regs., Part II. and the Staff Manual respectively. Title pages will be prepared in manuscript.

WAR DIARY
or
INTELLIGENCE SUMMARY.
(Erase heading not required.)

Army Form C. 2118.

Place	Date	Hour	Summary of Events and Information	Remarks and references to Appendices
	27th 28th 29th		Quiet. Work on defences. Training of 8 Lewis Gun teams carried on with in the	
			"Z".	
	30th		Order No. 177 issued. Without incident.	APP. 55
			STRENGTH 45 Off + 746 O.R.	

[illegible] Capt. & Adjt.
13 R. Fus.

D. D. & L., London, E.C.
(A7833) Wt. W593/M1672 350,000 4/17 Sch. 52a Forms/C/2118/14

A P P E N D I C E S

47A
48
49
50
50A
51
52
52A
53
54
55

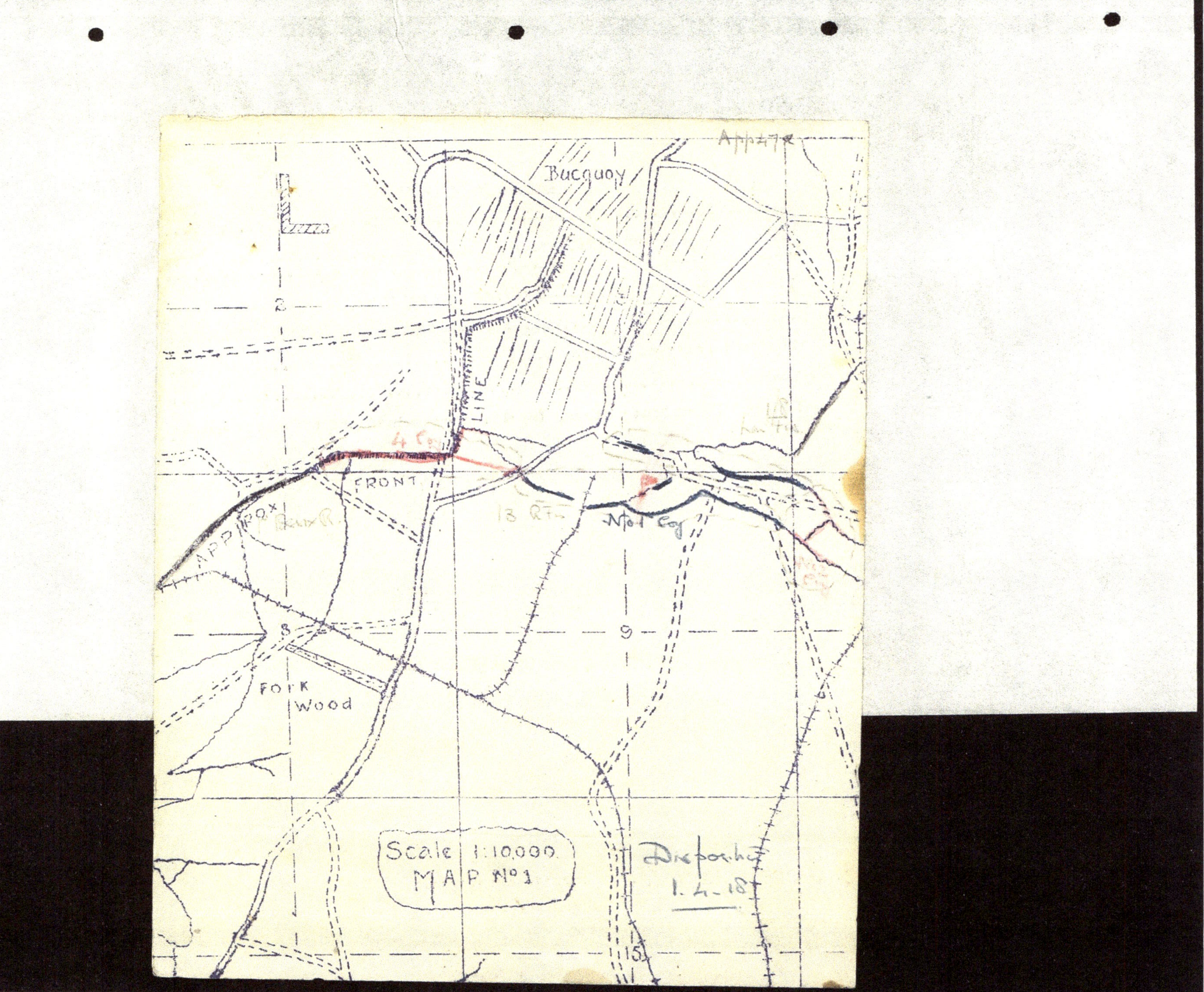

Bucquoy
LINE
4 Coy
FRONT
APPROX
13 R.F.
No 1 Coy
Fork Wood
2
8
9
15
Scale 1:10,000
MAP No 1
Despatched
1.4.18

SECRET.

App. 48

ORDER NO. 171.

Ref. Map - SHEET 57.D.N.E. 1/4/18.

---

1. The following readjustments will be made in the line to-night 2/3rd as soon as it is dark.

   (a) No 3 Coy. will take over No 2 Coy's line as far as trench junction at L.10.a.09.39.
   No 2 Coy. will continue to hold bombing block at L.10.a.2.3.

   (b) No 2 Coy. will take over No 1 Coy's line as far as trench junction L.9.b.00.72. (exclusive).

   (c) No 1 Coy. will take over No 4 Coy's line as far as L.3.c.2.1.

2. Moves will take place in the above order.

3. Completion of move will be notified to Battn. H.Q.

---ooo---

(sgd) GUY CHAPMAN,
Capt. & Adjt.
HARROW.

SECRET. **ROYAL FUSILIERS.** **ORDER NO. 172.**

APP 47

Ref. Map - SHEET 57D. n.e. 1/20,000. 4/4/18.

---

1. At a time & date to be notified later Brigade on right will attack & clear ROSSIGNOL WOOD establishing themselves on line K.17.b.10.75. along sunken road to K.12.d.65.30 - L.7.c.10.50 - L.7.a.45.00.

2. Attack will be carried out under an artillery barrage, & tanks may be used.

3. As soon as Bde. on right have established themselves on new line, the Battn. on right may attempt to gain ground on spur in L.7.d.

4. At ZERO hour a demonstration may be carried out by Stokes Mortars, either in No 2 Coys. or No 4 Coy's position, according to the wind with the object of screening the attack. Details will be issued later.

5. At ZERO hour the Battn. will demonstrate against enemy trenches in L.8.a. & b. with rifle & Lewis Gun fire & also deal with any enemy who may attempt to advance or retire across the open ground.

6. Reports will be forwarded as Os.C.Coys. deem advisable to Battn. H.Q.

(sgd) GUY CHAPMAN,
Capt. & Adjutant.
15th R.Fus.

Copy to No 1 Coy.
2 "
3 "
4 "

SECRET. J189.

App 50

To :- **Nos. 1, 2, 3 & 4 Coys.**

Z day is 5th April.

ZERO hour is 5.30 a.m.

(sgd) GUY CHAPMAN.

Capt. & Adjutant.

9.45 p.m.

4/4/18.

App. 50A

SHORT SUMMARY OF OPERATIONS AT BUCQUOY ON 5/4/18.

During the period 1/4th April enemy had shown little activity, but there were certain indications that this might be increased in the future, guns being hauled into position. etc.,

On the morning of the 4th a flight of heavy fighting machines flew over BUCQUOY dropping bombs, & during the afternoon trenches occupied by Nos. 1, 2 & 3 Coys. were subjected to a heavy bombardment, which afterwards proved to have been a practice bombardment for the attack.

On the morning of 5th April about 5.30 a.m. the enemy opened a heavy bombardment from E. & S. on battery positions. This bombardment coincided with an attack undertaken by the 63rd Infantry Brigade at ROSSIGNOL WOOD.at 6.3 0 a.m. the enemy extended the bombardment to cover whole front line system on the E. & S. of BUCQUOY, the village & squares L.3.c. - L.2.d. - L.2.b. also all communications. Bombardment was very severe, chiefly with 77mm and 105 mm.

Trenches held by No 1 Coy. were practically obliterated, but the casualties were fortunately not severe. On Nos. 2 & 4 Coys. line the enemy's shelling was not so accurate.

At 8.30 a.m. Right Company (No 4 Coy) reported enemy likely to attack. Information was passed to Battalion on the left & also to the Brigade.

At 8.45 a.m. the enemy's artillery lifted off front line & spasmodic attacks begun at various points. A small attack in L.9.a. & L.8.b. was easily beaten off with Lewis Gun & rifle fire. At same time the enemy made two strong bombing attacks up the trenches in L.10. towards two bombing posts, L.10.a.3.3. & L.10.a.3.5. held by No 2 Coy & No 3 Coy. respectively; this attack was easily beaten off, but the enemy succeeded in driving our post in at the former position as far as Coy. H.Q. at L.10.a.0.5. An immediate bombing attack undertaken by 2nd Lieut. H. Kirk, D.C.M. & No.4674 Sgt. Bowden H.R. ~~immediately~~ restored the position, the enemy retiring leaving several dead, including an officer. At the same time the enemy attacked in 3 waves from the E. about the Grid Line between L.4 & L.10. He was easily thrown back by Lewis Gun & rifle fire.

At 10 a.m. Nos.1 & 3 Coys. reported line intact & quite happy, but at same time men of the 1/8th Lancashire Fusiliers were found retiring on the Western side of BUCQUOY. On enquiry it was found that practically the whole of the 8th Lancashire Fusiliers had retired, with the exception of elements of their Right Company. Battalion H.Q. at once got into touch with Battn. H.Q. of the 8th Lancashire Fusiliers, who did not appear to be aware of the position, & after ~~wards there was~~ great difficulty. The position was to some extent re-organised & 8th Lancashire Fusiliers, under their Commanding Officer attempted to advance through the village, meantime however, the enemy had succeeded in pressing home his advantage & was already occupying the Eastern portion of the village as far as L.3.Central. This was about 10.40 a.m. A message was at once sent to Nos 2 & 3 Coys. as follows :-

> ' Enemy are reported to be in the village about cross-roads L.3.c.90.60. If position is such & Battn. on your left being withdrawn, withdraw through front line & take up position approximately on Sunken Road L.2.b.9.4. - L.3.c.00.40. '

At 12 noon No 4 Coy. was ordered to form their Support platoon on road between L.2.d.95.25 & cross roads L.3.c.05.85. Battn. H.Q. Details at same time extended Northwards from this point to cover Sunken Roads exit from this village. No 3 Coy. about this time ascertained that the whole of the 8th Lancashire Fusiliers, except about half a platoon, had evacuated the position & that enemy had occupied the Wood in L.3.d. - L.4.c. up to which point they had rushed several machine guns & trench mortars. No 2 Coy. at once commenced their withdrawal by way of Sunken Road L.9.b. - L.3.d. No 3 Coy. having destroyed their positions as much as possible by throwing bombs in dug-outs, etc., followed. Both retirements were covered by Support platoon of No 1 Coy. under 2nd Lieut. C.E.Vickers, M.M. This platoon got into position along the Southern bank of sunken road & engaged enemy in L.3.d.

The withdrawal of these 2 Coys. somewhat uncovered the left flank of No 1 Coy. who were rushed before they could get clear. Heavy fighting took place around the Coy. H.Q. L.9.b.1.8. which had been partially blown in with several men buried. Company were only able to extricate themselves at the cost of several men being taken prisoners. The Company Commander, A/Capt. J.K. Gwinnell, was also wounded about this time, but continued to control the retirement until eventually overcome by weakness.

At 2.0 p.m. position of Companies was approximately as follows :-

No 4 Coy. on Right in their original line with one platoon on the line L.2.d.99.22. - L.3.a.0.5. along sunken track. Line of the sunken track was continued by 2 platoons of No 1 Coy. - Battn. H.Q. Details & the carrying platoon under 2nd Lieut. G.S. Gibbons. North of this line No 2 Coy. re-organising, & took up a line in the orchards of N.W. corner of L.2.a. No 3 Coy. & 1 platoon No 1 Coy. occupied trench running from L.2.a.2.2. - L.2.a.6.8.

In the village, 2nd Lieut. R.K.Keller, 13th R.Fus. (attached 112th T.M.Bty) was holding on to an advanced position about cross roads L.3.a.85.35. with a group of Nos. 1 & 2 Coys. a few of 1/8th Lancashire Fusiliers & some of the

112th T.M.Bty.

Battn. H.Q. was withdrawn to L.2.a.2.2.

The enemy showed no signs of pressing home the attack, having secured the high ground in L.4. & 10.

Line was quickly re-organised, H.Q. Details were relieved by platoons of No 1 Coy. opposite late Battalion H.Q. & the whole of the 3 platoons No 1 Coy, & the carrying platoon under 2nd Lieut. G.S. Gibbons, were placed under command of Capt. L.F. Woodforde.

2.15 p.m. a small counter-attack had been in the meanwhile undertaken by 1/8th Lancashire Fusiliers, in which the C.O. & 2nd in Command were both killed.

At the same time 1/5th Lancashire Fusiliers were moved up into the gap on the left. About 4.0 p.m. a counter-attack was undertaken by this Battalion in which Nos 2 & 1 Coys. were ordered to conform, but were held up by heavy machine gun fire.

1/5th Lancashire Fusiliers also made little progress.

5.0 p.m. By this time the sunken road held by a platoon of No 4 Coy. had become untenable owing to heavy enfilade machine gun fire. The remainder of the platoon holding this line was therefore withdrawn. The line being adjusted as follows : L.2.d.27.21 - junction of road & trench L.2.d.40.72 No 4 Co., thence Eastwards a line of posts as far as cross roads L.3.c.05.85. thence to L.3.a.3.0, thence N.E. L.3.a.42.45, where the left flank of A Coy. of the 6th Bedfords, who had been sent forward in support, was established, in touch with 1/5th Lancashire Fusiliers.

No 3 Company in Support in trench running N. & S. in L.2.b. & d.

Enemy did not resume attack during night & the organisation & consolidation were carried out without interference.

During the 6th April further re-adjustments were made & No 3 Coy. relieved a Company of 6th Bedford Regiment.

Bucquoy
LINE
FRONT
APPROX
Fork
Wood
4
2
Scale 1:10,000
MAP No 1
57 D

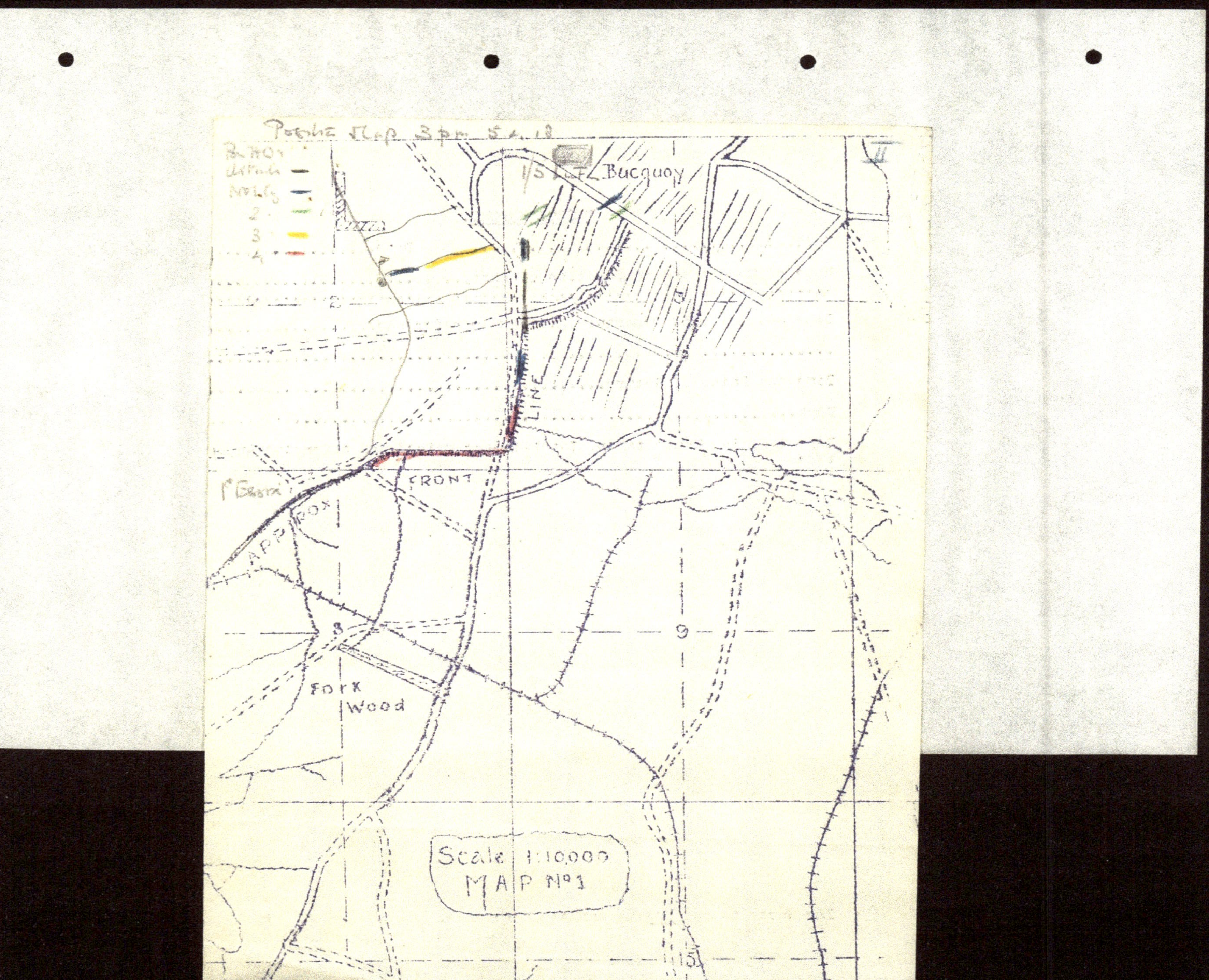

II
Bucquoy
LINE
FRONT
Fork
Wood
9
8
Scale 1:10,000
MAP No1

Bucquoy
LINE
FRONT
APPROX
Fork
Wood
Scale 1:10,000
MAP No 1
57D

SECRET.

ROYAL FUSILIERS. ORDER No. 173. App 51

Ref. Map - SHEET 57D. N.E. 1/20,000. 19/4/18.

---

1. The Battn. will be relieved by 8th Som. L.I. in Brigade Reserve to-night 9/10th.

2. GUIDES (2 per Coy) & 2 per Battn. H.Q.) will rendezvous at S.W. corner of PIGEON WOOD (E.30.a.0.3.) at 8.15 a.m.

3. List of any trench stores to be handed over will be sent to Battn. H.Q. by 3.0 p.m.

4. Completion of relief will be notified to Battn. H.Q. by runner.

5. On relief Battn. will move into Divisional Reserve in K.8.d. & K.14.b. relieving 3 Coys. 4th Australian Bde.

6. Coys. will move by ½ Coys. at not less than 100 yards distance. Route - E.28.d.5.2. FONQUEVILLERS - Road Junction E.26.d.6.2. where guides found by Rear Echelon will meet them.

7. TRANSPORT.- Limbers for Lewis Guns, etc., will be at road junction E.30.a. 95.55 at 8.45 p.m.

8. Companies will report arrival in new position together with location of Coy. H.Q.

(sgd) GUY CHAPMAN,
Capt. & Adjt.
13th R.Fus.

ISSUED at 9 a.m.

Copy to No 1 Coy.
2 "
3 "
Rear H.Q.
8th Som.L.I.
File.

SECRET. App. 52

13th Bn. ROYAL FUSILIERS. Order No. 174.

Ref. Sheet 57.D.N.E. 12/4/18.

---

1. Battn. will relieve 13th R.B. in the line from K.11.c.5.7. to K.11.b.50.95 to-night 12/13th as under :-
   - (a) No 1 Coy. relieves Right Front Coy. R.B. from K.11.c.5.7. - Sunken road K.11.b.1.5.(excl)
   - (b) No 3 Coy. relieves Left Front Coy. R.B. from Sunken road K.11.b.1.5. (incl) to K.11.b.50.95.
   - (c) No 2 Coy. relieves Support Coy. R.B. in K.11.a.15.70 - K.5.d.1.6.
   - (d) No 4 Coy. will move into line K.5.c.50.55 - K.10.b.90.95.
   - (e) Battn. H.Q. will be established at K.4.d.8.8.

2. Starting Point will be Road Junction E.26.d.65.20. Coys. will pass S.P. as under :-

   No 1 Coy.
   3 "
   2 "
   4 "
   Battn. H.Q.

   150 yards distance will be observed between platoons. Leading Coy. will pass starting point at 8.15 p.m.

3. Details of relief have been arranged between Os.C.Coys. concerned. Trench stores will be taken over as usual, duplicates of receipts forwarded to Batt. H.Q. with relief complete message.

4. Immediately on completion of relief, front line Coys. will establish liaison posts with the Battn. & Coys. on their flanks.

P.T.O.

5. Completion of relief will be notified to Battn. H.Q. K.4.d.8.8. by runner.

6. Transport.- (a) One limber for No. 1, 2 & 3 Coys. stores & Lewis Guns & one limber for No 4 Coys. & H.Q. will be at Battn. H.Q. at 7.15 p.m. These limbers will also carry 6 tins of water per Coy. & 8 for Battn.H.Q. Limbers will dump at K.4.d.8.8.

(b) Packs, blankets & Officers' kits will be collected as already notified, also cookers & watercarts.

(sgd) GUY CHAPMAN,
Capt. & Adjutant.

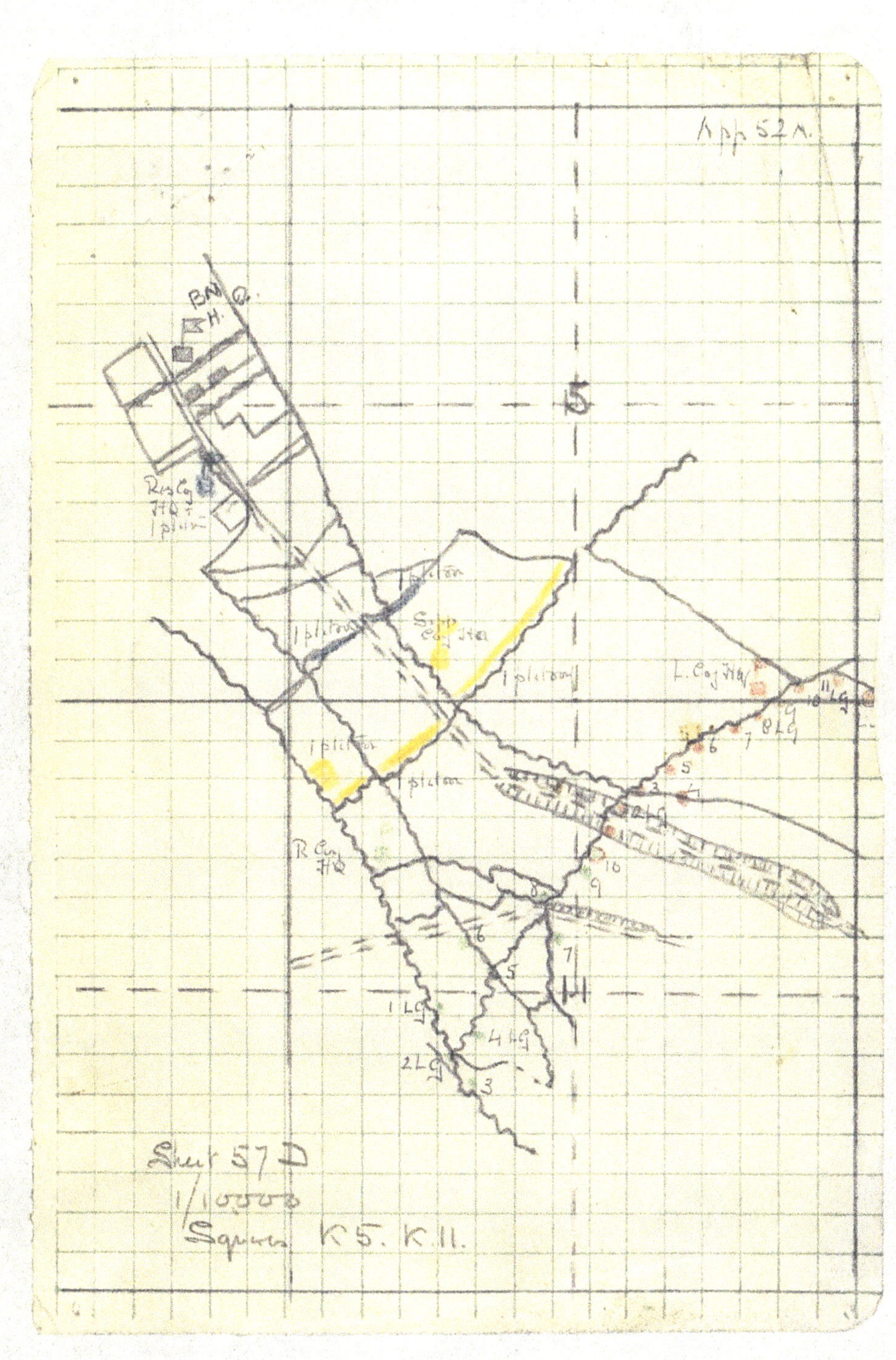

App 52A.
Bn H.Q.
Res Coy HQ + 1 pltn
1 pltn
1 pltn
1 pltn
1 pltn
1 pltn
L. Coy HQ
R Coy HQ
1 LG
2 LG
4 LG
8 LG
11 LG
5
11
Sheet 57 D
1/10000
Squares K5. K11.

13th Bn. Royal Fusiliers. **Order No. 175.** App 53

Ref. Sheet 57.D.N.E. 1/20,000.
57.D. 1/40,000.

15. 4. 18.

---

1. 1/5th Lancs. Fus. will relieve the Battalion in trenches to-morrow night 16/17th as under :-

A Coy. 5th L.F. will relieve Nos 2. & 4 Coys. (taking over No 2 Coy.H.Q.)
D Coy. " " " No 1 Coy. in Support.
C Coy. " " " No 3 " " Reserve.

2. Details of relief will be arrangedbbetween Os.C.Coys. concerned. Advance parties of 1 Officer & 2 N.C.O's 5th L.F. per Coy. 13th R.F. will report tonight to reconnoitre & take over line.

3. Guides will be found as under :-
For A Coy. 5th L.F. 3 guides per ½ Coy. & H.Q. by No 1 Coy.
2 " " ½ " by No 3 Coy.
D Coy. 5th L.F. 5 guides (one per platoon & one per Coy H.Q.) found by No 1 Coy.
C Coy. 5th L.F. 5 guides (one per platoon & one per Coy. H.Q.) by No 3 Coy.
B Coy. 5th L.F. 1 guide per Coy. H.Q. found by No 3 Coy.
No 3 Coy. will find an Officer to take charge of the guides. This Officer & the guides will report to Adjutant at Battn. H.Q. at 8.45 p.m. for instructions.

4. Protective patrols will cover the front during relief.

5. Trench stores, etc., will be handed over & receipts obtained, Receipts to be forwarded to Battn. H.Q. by noon 17th inst.

P.T.O.

6. Relief complete will be notified to Battn. H.Q. by wiring initial of surname of each O.C. Coy.

7. On relief, Battn. will move to BOIS-DE-WARNIMONT (I.17) one mile W. of ST. LEGER - LES - AUTHIE.
   Route : FONQUEVILLERS - CHAT de - la HAIE - BAYENCOURT - COIGNEUX - ST. LEGER.

8. Movement E. of SOUASTRE FORK (E.25.b.) will be made in bodies of no larger strength than platoons. 200 yards distance will be observed.

9. **Transport** : T.O. will arrange to have 2 limbers & a half limber at Battn. H.Q. at 9.45 p.m. for carriage of Lewis Guns, stores, etc. The following will be brought out of the line :-
   All new pattern Rifle Grenade Dischargers.
   All boxes No 36 Grenades.
   All petrol tins.
   All hot food containers, haypacks, or hot food, S.A.A. boxes.

10. Rear H.Q. will make all arrangements re billets at BOIS DE WARNIMONT, blankets & packs, hot food for Battalion on arrival in camp.

(sgd) GUY CHAPMAN,
Capt. & Adjutant,
13th R. Fus.

ISSUED at 10.45 p.m.

13th Bn. Royal Fusiliers. Order No. 176.

App 5H

Maps - [illegible] 57c. 1/40,000.
57c. [illegible] 1/20,000.

---

1. The Battalion will relieve 2/4th Duke of Wellington Regt. in the Reserve area to-night 24/25th.

2. Companies will relieve as under :-

No 2 Company will relieve one company 2/4th D. of W. R.Q. about [illegible].
No 4 Company will relieve one company 2/4th D. of W. R.Q. about [illegible].7.6.
No 3 Company will relieve one company 2/4th D. of W. R.Q. in about [illegible].4.c.5.8.
No 1 Company will relieve one company 2/4th D. of W. R.Q. in the [illegible].
Battn. H.Q. will relieve Battn. H.Q., D. of W. at the [illegible] ([illegible].13.c.6.[illegible])

3. Starting Point will be road junction 100 yards N. of [illegible]'s Stores.
Companies will pass starting point in the following order :-
No 4 Company.
2
3
H. Qrs.
No 1 Company.
Leading company will pass starting point at 5.30 p.m.
ROUTE will be road junction I.16.b.9.5. - Road Junction I.12.a.99. 20. - Road junction J.1.d.4.0. - Road junction [illegible] [illegible] - [illegible] CHURCH & junction of track & road [illegible].22.c.0.1.
Leading company will not pass road junction I.12.a.99.20 before 5.45 p.m.

4. [illegible].- 1 Officer & 3 O.R. per company, 1 Officer & 2 O.R. per H.Q. Coy. will meet Battalion at junction of track & road [illegible].22.c.0.1.

5. All movement will be made in file. [illegible] West of [illegible] Battn. will move by companies at [illegible] yards distance. East & N.E. of [illegible] movement will be by parties not larger than platoons at 200 yards distance.
Usual hourly halts will be observed.

6. [illegible].- Fighting Order. - Jerkins rolled & attached to belts by pack straps.

7. TRANSPORT.- Transport Officer will arrange to have 2½ limbers at disposal of Coys. going into the line as under :-

(a) 1 limber for Nos. 3 & 4 Coys. to dump at [illegible].7.6. [illegible] corner of [illegible] WOOD.

(b) Half limber for No 2 Coy. to dump at [illegible] corner of [illegible] WOOD.

(c) 1 limber for No 1 Coy. & H.Q. Company, dump at [illegible].27 to the [illegible].

(a) & (b) will move via [illegible] to [illegible].

(c) will move via [illegible] - [illegible] ([illegible].16.a.5.7.) to the [illegible].

Coys. will arrange to send a small off-loading party with limbers.
All material for trenches must be packed by 5.0 p.m.

8. [illegible].- All trench stores, defence schemes, trench maps, etc., will be taken over by relieving companies & forwarded to reach Bn. H.Q. by 9.0 a.m. 25th inst.

[illegible]

13th Bn. Royal Fusiliers. **Order No. 17[illegible].** APP 55

Ref 57D.N.E. 1/20,000. 30/4/18

---

1. The Battn. will relieve 8th Linc. R. in Right Sub-sector of Right Section to-morrow night 1/2nd May as under :-

   (a) No 2 Coy. will relieve D Coy. Lincs. R. on R.Front.
   (b) No 4 " " " C " " on L.Front.
   (c) No 1 " plus one platoon No 3 Coy. will relieve 'A' Coy. plus one platoon 'B' Coy. 8th Lincs. R. in Support.
   (d) No 3 " less one platoon will relieve 'B' Coy. less one platoon 8th Lincs. R. in Reserve.

2. Companies will leave present positions in order & at times stated below :-

No 2 Coy.	8.30 p.m.
4 "	8.40 p.m.
1 "	8.45 p.m.
3 "	9.0 p.m.
Battn. H.Q.	9.5 p.m.

3. GUIDES.- Guides will be at E. entrance to RETTEMOY FARM (F.25.c.40.85) Guides will be 3 per Coy. Post guides will be at respective Coy.H.Q.

4. Trench stores, defence schemes, etc., will be taken over from Coys. being relieved & receipts given. Duplicates of receipts will be ~~provide~~ forwarded to Bn. H.Q. by 6.a.m. 2nd inst.

5. Particular attention is to be given to the taking over of liaison posts with flank Battns. Os.C. Nos. 2 & 4 Coys. will ensure that such posts are thoroughly known before completion of relief.

6. Coys. will forward to Battn. H.Q. by 6.a.m. 2nd ~~inst~~.prox. sketch or report showing exact location of posts, etc., & positions of Lewis Guns.

7. RATIONS.- Q.M. will arrange with T.O. that rations for all Coys. & H.Q. for 2nd prox. are delivered at dump at the POPLAR, E.23.c.2.8. at 6.30 p.m. Coys. will send down on these limbers all petrol tins, cooking utensils not required, etc.

8. WATER.- (a) T.O. will arrange to have both watercarts at the POPLAR at 4.45 p.m. Coys. will fill tins here & fill waterbottles therefrom. These tins will be sent down on ration limbers at 6.30 p.m.
   (b) T.O. will deliver water (6 tins per Coy. & 1[illegible] fuel at N.W. corner of RETTEMOY FARM (E.30.d.49.78) at [illegible] p.m. Coys. will draw water & fuel from Provost Sgt. at Batt. H.Q. (E.30.d.99.70) after completion of relief.

9. COMMUNICATIONS.- Coys. will take over & use code calls of 8th Linc.R. on telephone up to M.N. 2/3rd prox. Battn. H.Q. will use call of 8th Lincs.R. (E.D.B.) when communicating with Coys.

10. Relief complete will be notified to Battn. H.Q. by wiring code word 'YES'. This will be confirmed by runner.

(sgd) GUY CHAPMAN,
Capt. & Adjt.

Copy to each O.C.Coy.
Rear H.Q.
T.O.
War Diary.

------

31 G.
(22 sheets)

WD 32

CONFIDENTIAL

WAR DIARY

OF

13TH. ROYAL FUSILIERS

From 1ST MAY 1918 to 31st. MAY 1918

(VOLUME 34)

Instructions regarding War Diaries and Intelligence Summaries are contained in F. S. Regs., Part II. and the Staff Manual respectively. Title pages will be prepared in manuscript.

WAR DIARY
or
INTELLIGENCE SUMMARY.
(*Erase heading not required.*)

Army Form C. 2118.

Place	Date	Hour	Summary of Events and Information	Remarks and references to Appendices
	May			
	1		Strength of Battalion 45 Officers 749 Other Ranks.	
	2 3		Battalion in line as per disposition Map attached.	App 54
	4		Inter-company relief - Order No. 178.	App 55.
	5		Weather good. Situation quiet but enemy attack expected.	
	6		Transport lines shelled by H.V. gun - Lieut. J. Marquard (Transport Officer) wounded.	
	7		2nd Lieut. F. Illing wounded while leading a patrol.	
			Capt. Cocke, American E.F. attached for instruction. Order No. 179 issued.	App 56
			Battalion relieved by 6th Bedford Regt. & withdrawn into close support.	
			Map attached. Lieut. & Q.Mr. L. Raven & T/2nd Lieut. H.J. Keeble joined Battalion.	App 57
	8-11		Battalion in close support.	
	9		2nd Lieut. F. Illing died of wounds.	
	10		The u/m were awarded decorations for gallantry in action during period 1 - 6th April, 1918 at BUCQUOY.	
			THE MILITARY MEDAL.	
			No. 19987 L/Cpl. H.L.L. Marrian.	
			205116 Pte A. Day.	
			5984 " C.J. Bond.	
			53198 " W.W. Walker.	
			27735 " A.W. Wilson.	

D. D. & L., London, E.C. (A7883) Wt. W8o3/M1672 350,000 4/17 Sch. 52a Forms/C/2118/14

Army Form C. 2118.

Instructions regarding War Diaries and Intelligence Summaries are contained in F. S. Regs., Part II. and the Staff Manual respectively. Title pages will be prepared in manuscript.

WAR DIARY
or
INTELLIGENCE SUMMARY.
(Erase heading not required.)

Place	Date	Hour	Summary of Events and Information	Remarks and references to Appendices
	May		THE MILITARY MEDAL.	
			No. 63381 Pte W.R. Siggers.	
			228112 " L. Fisher.	
			14285 Cpl. J. Dodkins.	
			66711 Pte A. Grafton.	
			BAR TO MILITARY MEDAL.	
			No. 2974 L/Cpl. W. Ormsby M.M.	
	12		Order No. 180 issued. Battn. relieved 1st Essex Regt. without incident. 2nd Lieut. A.E. Floyd wounded.	App. 57a
	13 to 17		Quiet tour. On night 14/15th. Battn. took over one company front from 6th Bedford Regt. Disposition as attached. Order No. 181.	App. 58, 59
			On night 16/17th a patrol under 2nd Lieut. C.E. Vickers, M.M. engaged a strong party of the enemy & after a sharp fight were forced to withdraw to our own line.	
	17		Order No. 182 issued. 2/7th West Yorks Regt. relieved Battn. Battn. withdrawn into reserve at LOUVENCOURT.	App. 60
LOUVENCOURT (SHEET 57D I. 34)	18		Sleeping & refitting.	
	19		Bathing & refitting.	
	20		Training commenced.	
	21		Training ended. 400 men on working party in neighbourhood of SAILLY-au-BOIS. Order No. 183 issued.	

D. D. & L., London, E.C. (A7833) Wt. W203/M1672 350,000 4/17 Sch. 52a Forms C/2118/14

Army Form C. 2118.

Instructions regarding War Diaries and Intelligence Summaries are contained in F. S. Regs., Part II. and the Staff Manual respectively. Title pages will be prepared in manuscript.

WAR DIARY
or
INTELLIGENCE SUMMARY.
(Erase heading not required.)

Place	Date	Hour	Summary of Events and Information	Remarks and references to Appendices
	May 21		The undermentioned Officers & N.C.O's were awarded decorations for gallantry in action near BUCQUOY 1 - 5th April :-	
			THE DISTINGUISHED SERVICE ORDER	
			T/Lieut-Col. R.A. Smith, M.C.	
			THE MILITARY CROSS.	
			T/Capt. L. F. Woodforde.	
			T/2nd Lieut. J. Davis.	
			THE DISTINGUISHED CONDUCT MEDAL.	
			No. 1712 Cpl. W. Muckell.	
			4674 Sgt. H. Bowden.	
			THE MILITARY MEDAL.	
			No. 229690 Sgt. A.N. Goodman.	
	22		Order No. 183 cancelled. Battn. manned RED LINE & were criticised by G.O.C., IV Corps.	App 61
	23		Battn. moved to camp at VAUCHELLES. Training resumed.	
	24		Training continued.	

D. D. & L., London, E.C. (A7883) Wt. W803/M1672 350,000 1/17 Sch. 52a Forms/C/2118/14

Instructions regarding War Diaries and Intelligence Summaries are contained in F. S. Regs., Part II. and the Staff Manual respectively. Title pages will be prepared in manuscript.

WAR DIARY
or
INTELLIGENCE SUMMARY.
(Erase heading not required.)

Army Form C. 2118.

Place	Date	Hour	Summary of Events and Information	Remarks and references to Appendices
	May			
	25		Training. 3rd Army Commander walked over parade ground.	
VAUCHELLES.	26		Training continued.	
			No. 229691 Sgt. C. COWLEY was awarded Military Medal for gallantry in action on 7/5/18 near BUCQUOY.	
	27		Training continued.	
	28		Training continued.	
	29		Training continued.	
	30		Division moved into G.H.Q. reserve.	
	31		Training continued.	
			Strength 45 Off. 795 O.R.	

[illegible] Capt + Adjt. f Lt. Col. Cdg. 13 R.F.

D. D. & L., London, E.C. (A8004) Wt. W1771/M2031 750,000 5/17 Sch. 52 Forms/C2118/14

52.G.
(14 sheets)

W 33

CONFIDENTIAL

WAR DIARY

OF

13TH BN. ROYAL FUSILIERS

From 1st June 1918 to 30th June 1918

VOLUME 35

Army Form C. 2118.

Instructions regarding War Diaries and Intelligence Summaries are contained in F. S. Regs., Part II. and the Staff Manual respectively. Title pages will be prepared in manuscript.

WAR DIARY
or
INTELLIGENCE SUMMARY.
(Erase heading not required.)

Place	Date	Hour	Summary of Events and Information	Remarks and references to Appendices
VAUCHELLES (SHEET 57D 1/40,000 I)	1/6/18		Strength of Battalion 45 Officers - 795 Other Ranks.	
			Training continued. 13th R.Fus. won 4 out of 6 events in 112th Inf. Bde. Boxing Competition.	
	2/6/18		Battn. Sports held.	
	3/6/18		Brigade Field Day.	
	4/6/18		Training. Battn. ordered to hold itself in readiness to move 5th inst.	
		9.30pm	Transport moved under darkness via ARQUEVES - PUCHEVILLERS - TALMAS to WARGNIES (Sheet 11, 1/100,000 D.6.)	
	5/6/18	9.45pm	Battn. moved by bus from VAUCHELLES to CAVILLON area under cover of darkness.	
BOUGAINVILLE (SHEET 62 E 1/40,000 O.21)	6/6/18	4.45am	Battalion debussed at BRIQUEMESNIL & marched to BOUGAINVILLE, where it billeted. Transport rejoined at BOUGAINVILLE. Still in G.H.Q. Reserve, but administered by XXII Corps.	
	7/6/18		Training continued.	
	8/6/18		Training continued. C.O. & Company Commanders reconnoitred ground held by French 37th Division near BOVES (62.D. T.7.)	
	9/6/18		Enemy attack in NOYON - MONTDIDIER sectors. Battn. held in readiness to move. Training continued.	

D. D. & L., London, E.C. (A7883) Wt. W807/M1672 350,000 4/17 Sch. 52a Forms C/2118/4

Instructions regarding War Diaries and Intelligence Summaries are contained in F. S. Regs., Part II. and the Staff Manual respectively. Title pages will be prepared in manuscript.

WAR DIARY
or
INTELLIGENCE SUMMARY.
(Erase heading not required.)

Army Form C. 2118.

Place	Date	Hour	Summary of Events and Information	Remarks and references to Appendices
	10/6/18		Battn. moved to CONTY area by French bus service 11 a.m. Owing to breakdown Battn. did not reach CONTY until 7.30 p.m. Meanwhile destination had been altered & Battalion billeted at LE BOSQUEL.	
LE BOSQUEL (SHEET 66F 1/40,000 K.29)			Picquets & sentry groups mounted under orders of French IX Corps.	
	11/6/18		Training continued. Battn. held in Corps Reserve with orders to hold the crossings of the NOYE between COTTENCHY & LA FALOISE (Sheet 66.E. B.7 - M.26) & high ground West of river. Crossing between JUMEL & COTTENCHY reconnoitred.	
	12/6/18		Brigade allotted sector JUMEL - LA FALOISE.	
			Crossings JUMEL - LA FALOISE reconnoitred.	
	13/6/18		Battn. moved under cover of darkness to HEBECOURT. Capt. E.H.Davie went to England for 6 months home duty.	
HEBECOURT (SHEET 66F 1/40,000 F2)	14/6/18		Battalion allotted second main line BOIS de GENTELLES - BOIS de BLANGY as counter-attack positions in the event of capture of the CACHY Plateau.	
			Battn. in Brigade reserve in T.5 & T.10 (Sheet 62.D.)	
	15/6/18		Nos. 1 & 2 Companies moved to DURY (Sheet 62.E. & G) in order to make room for 10th R.Fus. moving up into closer support. Order No. 183 issued.	App. 62
			Sectors in reserve to French re-allotted. 112th Inf. Bde. to hold 3rd position the NICHOLAS & GLISY SYSTEM (Sheet 62.D.S.W. Ed.2.a. Local) 13th R. Fus. in support in the GLISY SYSTEM. Defence Orders issued.	[signature] Lt-Col 13 R.F.

D. D. & L., London, E.C. (A7883) Wt. W803/M1672 350,000 1/17 Sch. 52a Forms C/2118/14

Instructions regarding War Diaries and Intelligence Summaries are contained in F. S. Regs., Part II. and the Staff Manual respectively. Title pages will be prepared in manuscript.

WAR DIARY
or
INTELLIGENCE SUMMARY.
(Erase heading not required.)

Army Form C. 2118.

Place	Date	Hour	Summary of Events and Information	Remarks and references to Appendices
	16/6/18		Training continued.	
	17/6/18		Training continued. Draft of 14 O.R. joined Battalion.	
	18/6/18		Training continued. Draft of 27 O.R. joined Battalion. Major C. Pratt, M.C., 2nd in Command, left for England on 6 months tour of home duty.	
	19/6/18		Warning order to move night 19/20th issued.	
	20/6/18		Order No. 184 issued. Battn. moved from HEBECOURT & DURY to NAMPS-au-MONT & billeted.	App. 63
			Order No. 185 issued.	App. 64
NAMPS-au-MONT	21/6/18	5.30AM	Battn. moved from NAMPS-au-MONT to LOEUILLY & entrained. Arrived at AUTHIEULE at 3 p.m. & billeted.	
AUTHIEULE 57 D.	22/6/18		Training continued. CHATEAU-de-la-HAIE SWITCH reconnoitred.	
	23/6/18		Order No. 186 issued.	APP. 65
	24/6/18		Addendum to Order 186 issued.	APP 66
	25/6/18	11 AM	Nos. 1, 3 & 4 Coys. moved to SOUASTRE by bus. Nos. 1 & 4 Coys. each sent 2 platoons to CHATEAU-de-la-HAIE SWITCH - Remainder of Battn. billeted in SOUASTRE. 2/5th W.Yorks Regt. relieved.	
		11.30AM	H.Q. & No 2 Coy. moved to SOUASTRE by bus.	
SOUASTRE	26/6/18		Order No. 187 issued. 2 remaining platoons No 4 Coy. relieved 2 platoons No 1 Coy.	APP 67
	27/6/18		Working Parties.	

[illegible signature]

D. D. & L., London, E.C. (A7883) Wt. W593/M1672 350,000 4/17 Sch. 52a Forms C/2118/14

Instructions regarding War Diaries and Intelligence Summaries are contained in F. S. Regs., Part II. and the Staff Manual respectively. Title pages will be prepared in manuscript.

WAR DIARY
or
INTELLIGENCE SUMMARY.
(Erase heading not required.)

Army Form C. 2118.

Place	Date	Hour	Summary of Events and Information	Remarks and references to Appendices
SOUASTRE	28/6/18		Working Parties.	
	29/6/18		Training.	
	30/6/18		Working Parties.	
			Strength of Battn. 41 Officer 827 Other Ranks.	

[signature] Lt. Col. Cmdg 13th

(A7883) D. D. & L., London, E.C. Wt. W203/M1672 350,000 4/17 Sch. 52a Forms/C/2118/14

CONFIDENTIAL

WAR DIARY

OF

13TH. BATTN. ROYAL FUSILIERS

FOR

JULY 1918

VOLUME 36

Vol 34

33 B. (15 file)

Instructions regarding War Diaries and Intelligence Summaries are contained in F. S. Regs., Part II. and the Staff Manual respectively. Title pages will be prepared in manuscript.

WAR DIARY
or
INTELLIGENCE SUMMARY.
(Erase heading not required.)

Army Form C. 2118.

Place	Date	Hour	Summary of Events and Information	Remarks and references to Appendices
SOUASTRE	1/7/18		Strength 41 Officers & 827 Other Ranks. Training carried out.	
	2/7/18		Order No. 188 issued. Battn. relieved 13th R. Bde. between L.8.a.00.65 & L.2.d.49.72 (Ref. Sheet 57.D.N.E.) with Battn. in RETTEMOY FARM. Relief without incident.	App. 68
	3/7/18		Without incident. Left Battn. on Divisional front projected gas into ABLAINZEVELLE. Enemy very quiet. Patrols saw nothing.	
	4/7/18		Quiet.	
	5/7/18		Quiet. Enemy put down small area shoot in L.1.b. L.2.a. during afternoon. A patrol entered enemy's posts at L.8.a.65.65 but met no enemy. Enemy has wired himself in well. 2nd Lieut. H.B. Wolferstan joined Battn.	
	6/7/18		X 70 issued. Battn. was relieved by 1/1st Herts R. & withdrawn into support.in PURPLE SYSTEM.	
	7/7/18		Without incident. Working parties.	
	8/7/18		Working parties.	
	9/7/18		Working parties.	
	10/7/18		Battn. relieved 1st Essex Regt. in left subsection - BUCQUOY Right Sector.	
BUCQUOY.	11/7/18		Without incident.	

D. D. & L., London, E.C. (A8004) Wt. W1771/M2031 750,000 5/17 Sch. 52 Forms/C2118/14

Instructions regarding War Diaries and Intelligence Summaries are contained in F. S. Regs., Part II. and the Staff Manual respectively. Title pages will be prepared in manuscript.

WAR DIARY
or
INTELLIGENCE SUMMARY.
(Erase heading not required.)

Army Form C. 2118.

Place	Date	Hour	Summary of Events and Information	Remarks and references to Appendices
	12/7/18	3.15 am.	Enemy attempted to rush 2 posts at L 2 c.10.84 - L 2 c 25 91. held by No 2 Coy. under cover of heavy barrage of 77mm on front & support lines, with a point barrage of 105 & 150 mm on rear lines. The enemy who are estimated to be about 80 strong got between & behind the posts. The party attacking M post were successfully dealt with by the Lewis gun team holding it & were forced to withdraw, leaving one prisoner (wounded, subsequently died) of 164 I.R. 111th Divn. in our hands. The party attacked O post apparently ran into their own barrage & withdrew of their own accord. Our casualties were Lieut. F.M. Sykes, Commanding No 2 Coy. wounded & 1 O.R. wounded.	
	13/7/18		8th Lincs. Regt. relieved Battn. Relief owing to casualties to Line transport not complete until 2.30 a.m. 14th. On relief, Bn. H.Q. Nos. 2 & 4 Coys. withdrew to SOUASTRE. Nos. 1 & 3 Coys. to CHATEAU-de-la HAIE Switch. Casualties during 11 days tour :- 1 Off. & 12 O.R. wounded, 1 O.R. killed. 2nd Lieut. T.J.C.Munford & 2nd Lieut. R.H. Peathey-Johns joined Battn.	
SOUASTRE	14/7/18		Working parties.	
	15/7/18		Working parties. Order No. 189 issued.	APP 69
	16/7/18		Working parties.	
	17/7/18		Working parties. Warning order to relieve 10th R.F. opposite ABLAINZEVELLE issued. Draft of 21 O.R. joined Battn.	
	18/7/18		Working Parties. Draft of 37 O.R. joined Battn. Order No. 190 issued.	APP 70
	19/7/18		Relief which should have taken place was cancelled owing to enemy having captured several of 13th K.R.R.C. & the consequent belief that they would inevitably give away the relief.	
TOP TRENCH F.21.d.a.6.	20/7/18		Battn. relieved 10th R.Fus. without incident in the left section of left Brigade sector - Front held by two Companies.	

D. D. & L., London, E.C. (A8004) Wt. W1771/M2031 750,000 5/17 Sch. 52 Forms/C2118/14

Instructions regarding War Diaries and Intelligence Summaries are contained in F. S. Regs., Part II. and the Staff Manual respectively. Title pages will be prepared in manuscript.

WAR DIARY
or
INTELLIGENCE SUMMARY.
(*Erase heading not required.*)

Army Form C. 2118.

Place	Date	Hour	Summary of Events and Information	Remarks and references to Appendices
	21/7/18		Nothing of importance. Bright moonlight hindered patrolling,	
	22/7/18		1st Berkshire R. raided on left. Fairly heavy shelling along left Coy. front & on support Coys. Draft of 35 O.R. joined Battn.	
	23/7/18		4th Msex. R. raided on right. There was little retaliation on our front. Order No. 191 issued.	APP. 71
F.19.a.4.8 SHEET 57D.NE	24/7/18		1st Essex Regt. relieved Battn. On relief, Battn. withdrew to support line - No 4 Coy. in BRADFORD TR. No 1 Coy. HALIFAX TR. No 3 Coy. in ESSARTS, No 2 Coy. in SAUSAGE TR. Bn.H.Q. at F.19.a.4.8.	
	25/7/18		Without incident. Working parties.	
	26/7/18		Without incident. Working parties. A draft of 29 O.R. joined Battn.	
	27/7/18		Without incident. Working parties. Weather bad.	
	28/7/18		Order No. 192 issued. Battn. relieved 1/1st Herts R. in Right subsector, left Brigade Front between L.3.b.20.75 & F.28.b.50.05.	APP 72
F.21.C.45.70	29/7/18		2nd Division raided in vicinity of AYETTE at 10.40 p.m. There was some retaliation on front line posts in L.3.b. & a. DURHAM TRENCH in F.27.b. Patrols worked forward by day into neighbourhood of BUCQUOY Cemetery & found enemy posts unoccupied & a bombtrap. 1 O.R. killed, 4 wounded.	
	30/7/18		Quiet. Order No. 193 issued.	APP. 73
	31/7/18	1.15am	1st Essex Regt. on immediate ~~right~~ left raided enemy in F.28.c & d. Enemy retaliated later, 2 O.R. wounded. Strength :- 40 Off. & 888 O.R.	

[signature] Lt. Col.

D. D. & L., London, E.C. (A8004) Wt. W1771/M2031 750,000 5/17 Sch. 52 Forms/C2118/14

34 B.
(20 st...)

112/37

WO 95/2135 (?)

WAR DIARY

OF

13th R. FUSILIERS

FOR MONTH OF

AUGUST 1918

VOLUME XXXVI

Instructions regarding War Diaries and Intelligence Summaries are contained in F. S. Regs., Part II. and the Staff Manual respectively. Title pages will be prepared in manuscript.

WAR DIARY
or
INTELLIGENCE SUMMARY.

(Erase heading not required.)

Army Form C. 2118.

Place	Date	Hour	Summary of Events and Information	Remarks and references to Appendices
N of BUCQUOY Ref. Sheet 57D NE	1/8/18		Order No. 194 issued. Battn. relieved by 4th M-sex Regt. without incident. On relief Battn. withdrew to Forward Battn. Area of Reserve Brigade, with Battn. H.Q. in the 'Z' (E.23.c.) Companies were distributed as follows - 2 Coys. in BEER TRENCH (E.22.c. & d.) 1 Coy. in RUM TRENCH (E.29.b. & E.24.c.) & one Coy. in E.24.b. & d. Coys. finding working parties.	App. 74.
Z Area E23	2/8/18		Without incident. Heavy rain.	
	3/8/18		Without incident. Order No. 195 issued.	App. 75
	4/8/18		Without incident. Battn. relieved by 1st Essex Regt. to VALLEY CAMP, SOUASTRE.	
SOUASTRE	5/8/18		Without incident. 2nd Lieuts. R.J. Bailey, M. Dundas and H.H. Taylor joined Battn.	
	6/8/18		Lieut-Col. R.A.Smith, D.S.O.,M.C. proceeded to C.O's Conference, 3rd Army S.O.S. Major T.J.E. Blake took over command.	
	7/8/18		Without incident.	
	8/8/18		Attack scheme with contact patrol carried out by Nos. 2 & 4 Coys.	
	9/8/18		Order No. 196 issued. Battn. relieved 10th R.Fus. in support to Right Brigade Sector in E.24.d. & E.30. No 4 Coy. was caught by enemy harassing fire about E.30.a.2.8. 4 killed & 4 wounded. Major T.J.E. Blake was also slightly wounded, but remained at duty.	App. 76.
PIGEON WOOD E30 & E24d	10/8/18		Working parties. Enemy's harassing fire has shewn a distinct increase.	
	11/8/18		Working parties. Order No. 197 issued.	App. 77

D. D. & L., London, E.C.
(A8001) Wt. W1771/M2031 750,000 5/17 Sch. 52 Forms/C2118/14

Instructions regarding War Diaries and Intelligence Summaries are contained in F. S. Regs., Part II. and the Staff Manual respectively. Title pages will be prepared in manuscript.

WAR DIARY
or
INTELLIGENCE SUMMARY.
(*Erase heading not required.*)

Army Form C. 2118.

Place	Date	Hour	Summary of Events and Information	Remarks and references to Appendices
PIGEON WOOD	12/8/18		Projected attack postponed 24 hours. Working parties.	
	13/8/18	6 am	Projected attack took place. No enemy retaliation.	
	14/8/18		News received that enemy was withdrawing on front of Division to South Line at 2 p.m. approx. L.8.a.5.7. - L.8.d.0.9. - L.13.b.8.8. - L.13.b.3.2. - L.13.d.5.1. - L.19.d.0.0. No withdrawal yet apparent on Brigade Front.	
	15/8/18		Order No. 198 issued. Battn. relieved 1/1st Herts Regt. in line between L.7.b.9.6. & L.2.d.3.7. Nos. 1 & 4 Coys. in front line. Situation obscure. 1st N.Z. Brigade hold line of trench L.8.c.4.0 - L.8.d.0.8. but have no touch with our right on this line. 1/1st Herts patrols were unable to get through wire. Wire thoroughly reconnoitred during night. Trench system in L.8.a. & L.2.c. apparently strongly held.	App 78
SW of BUCQUOY	16/8/18		Orders received to attack & consolidate trenches in L.8.a. & L.2.c. Order No. 199 issued. Bombardment carried out in accordance with programme.	App 79
		6.15pm	Nos. 1 & 4 Coys. attacked. No 4 Coy. on left reached their objective. No 1 Coy. with the more difficult task, were able to oversome slight hostile opposition.	
		6.35pm	All objectives reported taken & patrols pushing forward.	
		9.0pm	Line L.8.b.8.2. - l.8.b.8.7. - L.3.c.0.2. occupied without difficulty & post line established. Patrols pushed out. Touch found at points on both flanks. No 3 Coy. moved from RETTEMOY FARM to WASP & KEANE TRENCHES. No 2 Coy. from N.W. of RETTEMOY FARM into CHUB TRENCH & RETTEMOY FARM. Enemy artillery active on trenches in L.8.a.& b.	
✓	17/8/18		Re-organisation & consolidation. Line of main PUISIEUX - BUCQUOY Road made good and patrols pushed out as far as RAILWAY in L.9.a. Enemy artillery moderately active on post line.	
	18/8/18		Patrols pushed out to trenches in L.9.b. during day. Battn. ordered to take over right company of 1st Essex Regt. on left. After some difficulties relief successfully carried out by 2.15 a.m. 19th. Disposition as shewn.	

D. D. & L., London, E.C.
(A8001) Wt. W1771/M2031 750,000 5/17 Sch. 52 Forms/C2118/14

Instructions regarding War Diaries and Intelligence Summaries are contained in F. S. Regs., Part II. and the Staff Manual respectively. Title pages will be prepared in manuscript.

WAR DIARY
or
INTELLIGENCE SUMMARY.
(Erase heading not required.)

Army Form C. 2118.

Place	Date	Hour	Summary of Events and Information	Remarks and references to Appendices
SW of Bucquoy	19/8/18		Quiet day. 8th Mx. Regt. relieved Battn. which withdrew to "Z" area. Batt. H.Q. E.23.c.5.4. Order No. 200 issued.	App 80
	20/8/18		Order No. 201 issued. Battn. moved into position.	App 81
	21/8/18		Zero was at 4.45 a.m. The Battn. moved on to its objective and consolidated positions. Casualties :- Capt. L.F. Woodforde, M.C. wounded ; Other Ranks - 3 killed 9 wounded. During the afternoon the Battn. was withdrawn into position W of HENLEY HILL & was disposed as follows :- No. 1 Coy. BUCQUOY AVENUE, F.25.b. 2 " LEEDS TRENCH F.26.a. 3 " LEEDS TRENCH F.25.b. & F.26.a. 4 " LEEDS TRENCH F.26.c. Battn. H.Q. was at F.25.b.9.1. This relief was complete by 9 5 p.m.	
W of Bucquoy.	22/8/18		During morning necessary details of re-organisation were carried out. Reconnoitring parties were sent forward to ACHIET-LE-PETIT. 2nd Lieut. R.H. Peathey-Johns wounded.	
		5.30pm	Verbal orders received for Battn. to move.	
		9.30pm	Battn. moved off into positions	
N of Achiet-le-Petit. Sheet 57C NW.	23/8/18	1.30am	Battn. in position with 4th BEDFORD REGT. A certain amount of difficulty was experienced owing to lack of accomodation. Operation orders were received from the 112th Inf. Bde.	
		9am	A conference of Coy. Commanders was immediately called & order No. 202 issued.	App 82
		11am	Attack commenced.	
		12.45pm	Objective gained & consolidated. T/Lieut.(A/Capt.) J. Marguard - killed. 2nd Lieutenants H. Kirk, D.C.M., C.E. Vickers, M.M., A.A. Allen, M.C., H.H. Taylor, P.R. Mills - wounded. Battn. H.Q. was established at G.16.a.1.8.	
SE of Achiet-le-Grand		5.5pm	Orders received for further advance & Order No. 203 issued.	App 83
		5.30pm	The second attack commenced but the barrage being put down 700 yards in front of position no headway was made.	

D. D. & L., London, E.C.
(A8001) Wt. W1771/M2031 750,000 5/17 Sch. 52 Forms/C2118/14

Army Form C. 2118.

Instructions regarding War Diaries and Intelligence Summaries are contained in F. S. Regs., Part II. and the Staff Manual respectively. Title pages will be prepared in manuscript.

WAR DIARY
or
INTELLIGENCE SUMMARY.

(Erase heading not required.)

Place	Date	Hour	Summary of Events and Information	Remarks and references to Appendices
SE of Achiet-le-Grand.	23/8/18	6.15pm	The Battn. returned to its original objective. 2nd Lieut. A. McCarthy - killed. During the evening the 8th Bn. Somerset L.I. passed through the Battn. & occupied trench runni from G.16.d.48.72. to G.17.a.3.5. Detailed account of day's operations appended.	App 84
	24/8/18		At dawn the 8th Bn. Somerset L.I. moved forward & the Battn. occupied the position vacated by them. Later, when it became evident that British troops had occupied BIEFVILLERS strong posts were established on the line G.22.b.35.80. - G.17.d.40.55. Orders were then received for the Battn. to move on to the rough general line G.12.c.1.7.- G.18.a.1.0. Order No. 204 issued.	
E of BIHUCOURT		6.30pm 8pm	Battn. established on new line. Lieut.Col. R.A. Smith, D.S.O.,M.C. resumed command of the Battn.	App 85
	25/8/18		The day passed without incident except that Battn. H.Q. moved forward to G.10.d.65.05. & later during the evening to G.12.c.25.20.	
	26/8/18		Day spent in improving positions & accomodation. Casualties from 21st - 26th inclusive :- Other Ranks 45 killed, 172 wounded, 7 Missing.	
	27/8/18		Day passed in improvising baths & general re-organisation. Slight shelling with H.V. H.E. & Shrapnel.	
	28/8/18		Line further advanced in front but Battn. disposition not altered.	
	29/8/18		Day quiet.	
	30/8/18		Normal training parades carried out.	
	31/8/18		2nd Lieut. N.E. LAMB joined Battn. with a draft of 100 Other Ranks. Strength of Battn. 35 Officers & 791 Other Ranks.	

D. D. & L., London, E.C.
(A8001) Wt. W1771/M2031 750,000 5/17 Sch. 52 Forms/C2118/14

[illegible signature] Lt Col
13th R. W. Fusiliers

App 84

13th Bn. The Royal Fusiliers.

REPORT ON THE OPERATIONS ENGAGED IN ON AUGUST 23rd, 1918.

On the 22nd inst. in accordance with orders received the Battalion moved up from its position West of HENLEY HILL to the position occupied by the 4th BEDFORDS in G.8. A certain amount of difficulty was experienced in getting the Coys. into position owing to the nature of the defensive line & the apparent disorganisation of the unit holding the line. The left flank of the left front company was considerably in rear of the general line being thrown well back.

At 9.0 a.m. 23rd inst. operation order No. GA1 was received from 112 Bde. & on these orders the Battn. operation orders were written & handed to Company Commanders at the conference.

At Zero hour the Battalion moved into its forming up line (road running N.E. through G.8.d. - G.9.a.) & formed up as follows :-

No 2 Company Capt. Whitehead, M.C.	Left Front.	No 3 Company. Lt.Marquard.	Right Front.
No 4 Company. 2/Lt.Allan, M.C.	Left Support.	No 1 Company. 2/Lt.Balley.	Right Support.

The left Coys. as anticipated experienced a certain amount of difficulty in getting their left flanks on to the road which was the Battalion's left boundary, but despite the distance to go & a small amount of M.G. fire, the Battn. was formed up & moved off punctually at Zero + 8, when the barrage lifted forward. Considerable opposition was met with from the BRICKWORKS & the trench running S.E. through G.9. G.15. G.16. (named BAPAUME TRENCH) both rifle & M.G. fire increasing as the Battn. advanced. At one time it appeared that the left might be seriously hung up, but parties were detailed to work round the N. & S. flanks of the BRICKWORKS while intense Lewis gun fire was brought to bear frontally on to the centre of resistance. This manoeuvre effectually disposed of the enemy resistance, & when he saw his flank had been turned, over 60 surrendered (in the area G.9.b. & c.) & eleven light machine guns were afterwards noted & marked.

In the meantime the right flank of the Battalion had pushed forward encountering a little resistance from BAPAUME Trench & from M.G. situated on the S. side of the road in G.9.c. & d. The left Coys. were immediately pressed forward to catch up to the barrage & to gain touch on the flanks, the line being reorganised & reformed with considerable skill while it was on the move forward. At Zero + 30 the whole Battalion was East of the road in G.9.c. & d. & Battn. H.Q. was temporarily established at the junction of trench and road at G.9.d.1.2. At Zero + 34 large parties of prisoners in fours were observed coming in from the direction of the village & left flank, & it was when they were at G.9.d.1.2. that the enemy turned his M.G. on to them, killing & wounding no inconsiderable number. The remainder (which contained some officers) were directed to Rear Battn. H.Q. without escort. The advance was continued with all speed, touch being established on the left, but no troops could be definitely established on the right flank. The attack was pressed forward with vigour, small pockets of the enemy with light M.G. making but feeble resistance; & at Zero + 45 the furthest advanced troops of the Battn. were observed crawling up the railway embankment. Directly the attacking waves came into view an intense rifle & machine gun fire was opened by the enemy, who were lining the top of the W. side of the cutting, & the advance was for the time being checked owing to casualties. The fire brought to bear on the attacking troops was of the severest nature & it was extremely difficult to locate with any exactitude where the main opposition was coming from. Many of the enemy were seen moving about on top of the cutting, but only fleeting glimpses could be obtained as they made full use of the natural cover provided. It was here that the men used their rifles & Lewis guns with good effect & strove to obtain superiority of fire against a well concealed enemy, & it was due to the big volume of fire developed (assisted by the trench mortars) that small parties of men were enabled to crawl forward & establish themselves on the crest of the cutting & so bring enfilade fire to bear on the enemy. It was at this same juncture that a Lewis gun team did magnificent work. The undergrowth on the left flank was not so dense

& this team rushed up the bank - across the rails - & up the E. bank of the cutting. Here they faced about & brought their gun into action, firing into the backs of the enemy & spraying the shelters & hutments in the bottom of the cutting.

Unfortunately all the team were picked off one by one, but this move temporarily disorganised the enemy. It was then seen that the enemy were retiring across the cutting some 800 yards on the right flank & fire was developed with success against this party & at the same time a platoon moved down under cover of the bank & rushed the enemy. This combination of events took the enemy by surprise & they at once began to hold up their hands, while the remainder of the Battn. made good the crest. The whole cutting was alive with Germans. Dug-out after dug-out was cleared, one large dug-out contained what was either the Staff or the Battn. Commander's Staff, & one of the German Officers who could talk English expressed his willingness to help & went round with the mopping up parties & ordered his own troops to come out & surrender, which they did with enthusiasm. The total amount of prisoners captured by the Battalion in the cutting was at the most conservative estimate 400, together with many heavy & light M.G's. These latter were found on both sides of the cutting in action, but there were many which had not been in action, as they were stacked together, probably for cleaning purposes. It is estimated that 15 trench mortars (light) were taken in the cutting, but no definite figures can be given as the Battalion moved on to its objective at once. It was obvious that the Battalion had taken the garrison by surprise, as there was ample evidence of a meal having been just prepared & hot coffee was steaming on the tables. While the mopping up was being completed, & the prisoners formed up & sent back, the two front Coys. had reorganised on the Eastern side of the cutting & were advancing towards their objective, being in touch with the K.R.R.C. on the left. As far as could be ascertained there were none of our troops in the immediate vicinity of the right flank, so orders were issued for a platoon of the front Coys. to move down the railway to clear up the situation. This platoon patrolled the railway line to the right flank for a distance of 1000 yards into G.15.d. headed by an Officer on a captured bicycle, but nothing was seen of either the enemy or our own troops.

The cutting was definitely crossed & the advance recommenced at Zero + 90, & Battn. H.Q. was established at G.16.a.1.8. at that time. Our troops advanced without further difficulty & took up positions in the trench running N.E. through G.16.a. which had apparently also been hurriedly evacuated. Two tanks were cruising about & one was asked to look after the right flank until the Battalion had reorganised in depth. Two light T.M's & three M.G's were captured in the trench.

Posts were established on the railway & a strong post at G.16.c.3.8. & Battn. H.Q. moved up to G.16.a.3.2. where it remained thereafter.

It was not possible to establish a line on the Battalion's objective, as the barrage did not lift from it until Zero + 136, at which time the 1/1st HERTS were to pass through, but no difficulty was experienced in establishing the objective when the barrage lifted.

The line then ran - Main line of resistance (2 Coys.) in trench & on railway in G.16.a. - posts on the general line G.16.c.3.1. - G.16.b.3.4. & one Coy. in reserve at Battn. H.Q. G.16.a.3.2.

Touch was established the whole time on the left, but the Battn. had been out of touch for a considerable period on the right. It was thought that this might not be as serious as it at first looked, as operation orders had laid down that the ESSEX would move straight forward & not halt with the Bn. refacing their left flank to the barrage, but patrols were pushed out the whole time & a Coy. kept in reserve to counter any offensive move on part of the enemy.

At Zero + 180 (approx.) two platoons (about) of the 1/1st HERTS appeared & it was thought that this regiment had turned up to go through the line. In the meantime our patrols had pushed out well to the front, but had not returned. At 2.40 p.m. the following message was received from the O.C., 10th R. Fus. :-

> " Our right Coy. is being held up by M.G. at G.16.d.50.40. & in Gun spur at G.16.d.50.70. As this is behind your front could you deal with it please . "

The area mentioned in the above message was of course well in front of our objective, on which we had been firmly established for some time, & should have been taken by the 1/1st HERTS, but on receipt of the message further patrols were pushed out & an Officer sent out to the flank near to endeavour to gain information. At 3.0 p.m. the patrols returned & reported that they had been heavily fired on from the direction of the Gun spur, & it was then definitely established that certain elements of the 1/1st HERTS had apparently passed through on the right flank & were then in the trenches in and about G.16.c.0.7. & claimed to be in touch with the ESSEX Regt.

A runner was sent to find the Officer in charge of the party of HERTS, & in the meantime the Battalion was "stoodto" ready to advance further. It may be said, in passing, that the Battalion could have advanced easily with a barrage at Zero + 136 & established itself on K line.

Patrols were again pushed out in front & to endeavour to gain touch with the 10th R.Fus. till it was clear what the 1/1st HERTS proposed to do & at 5.5 p.m. orders were received to advance & establish on a line G.29.a.8.8. - G.23.Central - G.18.c.4.4.

It is to be noted that the barrage was to open 300 yards in advance of final objective (K line) which was 500 - 600 yards in advance of the position held by the Battalion. & it was definitely known that the intermediate area was strongly held with enemy M.G's.

The attack was organised in two waves & one platoon was detailed to work up along the line of the railway & BAPAUME Trench. The attacking waves had only progressed about 200 yards when the enemy opened heavy fire right along the line. It was at once seen that it was impossible to move forward in any strength without artillery or tank support, & the Battalion had to withdraw to its original line. The platoon on the right actually succeeded in penetrating into the spinney & put some of the enemy to flight & killed the gun team, but had to withdraw & brought back valuable information as to the General dispositions.

At 6.15 p.m. the Battalion was on its original objective & organised in depth.

The total amount of prisoners passed through the Battalion Collecting Post amounted to over 1000, collected from all units. Receipts were obtained for over 500 prisoners all taken by this Battalion, & over 100 were used by M.O. for carrying purposes. The M.G's were not counted as the Bn. moved forward from the Rly.cutting & remained forward.

Appendix.

(i) It should be mentioned that the two light T.M's captured in the trench in G.16.a. were brought into action against the enemy's position in the trench specially mentioned above & a barrage was put down on these points when the battn. advanced at 5.30 p.m.

(ii) Trench Mortar was allotted to & followed the left supporting Coy. with orders to assist in breaking down the expected resistance at the BRICKWORKS & the Rly. cutting. Full use was made of the gun & when the Battn. arrived at its objective the section was withdrawn & kept in reserve, having done valuable work.

(iii) MACHINE GUNS. It was arranged that the section of M.G's attached to the Battn. should come into action from behind the forming up line & put down a standing barrage on the railway cutting until zero - 36 when it would lift on to the Battn's objective. This was done & when the cutting had been crossed, a message was sent back for the section to advance. The guns were then placed in a defensive position on the right & exposed flank so as to be able to sweep the covered approaches which existed & also to give assistance in case of any threatened frontal attack. These orders were carried out satisfactorily & the presence of these guns lent added security to the flank that was at one time in the air.

App 85

13th Battalion Royal Fusiliers.
Order No. 204.

SECRET.
24/8/18

Ref. map Sheet 57C N.W. 1/20,000

---

1. Each Coy. will carry up its own water supply.

2. An extra 50 rounds per man will be carried & as many bombs as possible. These will be made into dumps directly the Companies take up their new positions.

3. Companies will move off at once & take up their new positions on the rough general line G.12.c.1.7. to G.18.a.1.0. No.1 Coy. on right.

4. A representative of Headquarters Lieut. BURROWS has gone ahead to take over a Battn. H.Q. which will be notified later.

5. Reports to CROSS ROADS G.11.d.6.3. until Bn. H.Q. is established.

(sgd) E.S. HART, 2nd Lieut.
A/Adjutant.

ISSUED at 4.30 p.m.

Instructions regarding War Diaries and Intelligence Summaries are contained in F. S. Regs., Part II. and the Staff Manual respectively. Title pages will be prepared in manuscript.

WAR DIARY
or
INTELLIGENCE SUMMARY.
(Erase heading not required.)

Army Form C. 2118.

112/37 13 RF

98 36

Place	Date 1917	Hour	Summary of Events and Information	Remarks and references to Appendices
SHEET 57C BIHUCOURT	Sept 1		Strength of Battalion 35 Off. 791 O.R.	
			Battn. in recaptured camp & bivouacs in G.12.c. G.18.a & C. G.17.b. & d. Normal routine carried out.	
	2		Without incident.	
	3		Warning received that the battalion would move forward to relieve 16th Bn. Royal Warwickshire Regt. also a later report that the enemy had withdrawn.	
FAVREUIL		2.30PM	Battn. moved to valley in H.9.c. Order No. 205 issued.	App. 86
			C.O's conference was called & details of relief & subsequent advance explained. These were then communicated to all officers at a conference.	
		6.0PM	Battn. moved off & marched through FAVREUIL, FREMICOURT & LEBUCQUIERE. Tracing shows position taken over.	App. 87
E of VELU + S of HERMIES	4	1.30AM	Relief reported complete & without incident. Order No. 206 issued.	App. 88
		7.0AM	The battalion had formed up in sunken road in J.29.c. & J.35.a & moved forward. After proceeding about 200 yds. Machine gun fire was opened from J.36.d. & K.31.c. The right company was also subjected to Trench Mortar fire from these locations.	
			The advanced enemy machine guns were forced to retire by our fire & the Trench Mortar put out of action. Our advance was continued & one platoon crossed the canal at K.31.a.0.2. At this stage the battalion on the right were 500 yards in rear & it became necessary to delay the advance on account of the enemy machine gun cross fire from their front, until they came up in line. Two platoons were then pushed forward on to the railway in K.31.b.	35

D. D. & L., London, E.C. (A7883) Wt. W803/M1672 350,000 4/17 Sch. 52a Forms/C/2118/14

Army Form C. 2118.

Instructions regarding War Diaries and Intelligence Summaries are contained in F. S. Regs., Part II. and the Staff Manual respectively. Title pages will be prepared in manuscript.

WAR DIARY
or
INTELLIGENCE SUMMARY.
(Erase heading not required.)

Place	Date	Hour	Summary of Events and Information	Remarks and references to Appendices
S. of HERMIES	4		& K.32.a. north of the canal, & a Lewis Gun post established on Yorkshire Bank. The right company were again out of touch on their right & when it became evident that the 1st Herts could not move forward & small bodies of the enemy were seen moving up in K.32.a. our right was withdrawn & liaison established in tunnel under the canal in K.31.b.40.30. The movements of the left company were entirely dependent on the right. Similar M.G.fire was encountered & the line finally consolidated in Maxwell Avenue & in front of SQUARE COPSE. Touch was not gained with the 2nd Div. until the evening when they conformed to our line. The support & reserve Coys. occupied JUNO TRENCH & sunken road in J.36.b.	
			Battn. H.Q. was established at J.35.a.25.45.	
			Casualties - Officers : 2nd Lieut. C.W. Randall, " W.F. Burrows, " N.E. Lamb, A/Capt. H.W.Daniel,M.C. } Wounded.	
			Other Ranks : 20 killed 72 wounded.	
	5		Patrolling was carried out & outposts pushed forward, & the line consolidated in depth. Active hostile shelling with light guns & blue cross gas shells. During the evening No 2 Coy. took over CHEETHAM RESERVE as far as the junction with HENLEY AVENUE J.31.b.05.35. with two platoons in the outpost line.	
	6		During the night a patrol reconnoitred YORKSHIRE BANK and found it unoccupied. In consequence posts were established on its western edge, also in KITTEN TRENCH. The latter was forced to withdraw as the result of an enemy counter-stroke & took up a position at the junction of HENLEY AVENUE & CHEETHAM SWITCH, gaining touch with the 8th LINCOLN Regt. on the right.	

D. D. & L., London, E.C. (A7833) Wt. W803/M1672 350,000 4/17 Sch. 52a Forms/C/2118/14

Instructions regarding War Diaries and Intelligence Summaries are contained in F. S. Regs., Part II. and the Staff Manual respectively. Title pages will be prepared in manuscript.

WAR DIARY
or
INTELLIGENCE SUMMARY.
(Erase heading not required.)

Army Form C. 2118.

Place	Date	Hour	Summary of Events and Information	Remarks and references to Appendices
	7		Relief by 1st ESSEX Regt. Order No 207 issued.	app. 89
E. of VELU			Battn. moved to area J.28.c. J.33.b. J.34.a. & c. Battn. H.Q. J.27.d.6.6. Major T.J.E. Blake took over command of 1st ESSEX Regt.	
	8		Reorganization of companies.	
BEUGNY	9		Battn. moved to BEUGNY area. Order No. 208 issued.	app. 90
	10		No. 14425 Sgt. GIBSON W.J. MM. awarded bar to Military Medal. Refitting, & training of Lewis Gunners carried out.	
E. of VELU	11		Order No. 209 issued. Heavy enemy shelling of roads by H.V. guns. Battn. H.Q. J.27.d.6.6 Order No 210 issued.	app. 91 app. 92
	12		Draft of 146 O.R. joined Battn. in forward area.	
			Order No. 211 issued.	app. 93
	13		Without incident.	
BILHEM	14		Order No. 212 issued. Battn. under orders of G.O.C., 111th Inf. Bde. Relief complete without incident. After relief, order No. 213 issued & Battn. prepared for counter-attack. Counter preparation was fired at intervals during this period of anticipation.	app. 94 app. 95
	15		Order No. 214 issued & relief completed without incident. Battn. again under orders of G.O.C., 112th Inf. Bde.	app. 96
			Without incident.	

D. D. & L., London, E.C.
(A8001) Wt. W1771/M2031 750,000 5/17 Sch. 52 Forms/C2118/14

Army Form C. 2118.

Instructions regarding War Diaries and Intelligence Summaries are contained in F. S. Regs., Part II. and the Staff Manual respectively. Title pages will be prepared in manuscript.

WAR DIARY
or
INTELLIGENCE SUMMARY.

(Erase heading not required.)

Place	Date	Hour	Summary of Events and Information	Remarks and references to Appendices
BILHEM	17		Inter-company relief. Order No. 215 issued.	App. 97
			Order No. 216 was then issued for a minor operation. Instructions were given verbally & confirmed by this order. All necessary material was delivered & blocks B. & C. constructed by mid-night.	App. 99
	18		Zero was at 5.20 a.m. & the assault commenced at 5.40 a.m. The weather conditions were adverse & on account of strong belt of wire in position no surprise could be affected. The enemy was holding bombing blocks in Bass & Burton Lanes strongly. These had not been knocked out by artillery fire & in consequence no headway was made. Three successive attacks were made but were equally unsuccessful. Thereafter the attempt ceased & the line remained as formerly.	
			Casualties : Lieut. M.N. Wilcock. Killed. O.Ranks : 5 Killed & 19 wounded.	
		11AM	Warning order received re relief & order No 217 issued. Relief was completed without incident & Battn. H.Q. was established at P.2.d.2.6.	App. 99
BERTINCOURT	19		Day devoted to reorganization & interior economy. 2nd Lieuts. J.F.Keefe, H.A.R. Puttee, E.W. Parker,M.C. J.R.Talbot, E.L. Carter,M.M. H. Caldwell, D.E. Watt, E.M.Rees joined Battn.	

D. D. & L., London, E.C.
(A8001) Wt. W1771/M2031 750,000 5/17 Sch. 52 Forms/C2118/14

Instructions regarding War Diaries and Intelligence Summaries are contained in F. S. Regs., Part II. and the Staff Manual respectively. Title pages will be prepared in manuscript.

WAR DIARY
or
INTELLIGENCE SUMMARY.
(Erase heading not required.)

Army Form C. 2118.

Place	Date	Hour	Summary of Events and Information	Remarks and references to Appendices
BERTINCOURT	20		Order No. 218 issued. The u/m other ranks awarded the Military Medal :- 4860 Sgt. WING H.C.(K/A) 10934 Sgt. WHITTAKER A. 49322 Sgt. Campbell P. 4725 Cpl. FARLEY W.A. 7423 L/C. STEVENSON J.F. 59338 L/C. LAWRENCE C. (W/A) 17632 Pte LYDDIATE A. 63621 Pte SMITH H.J. (W/A) 228109 Pte BENNETT T.W. 63358 " WILLIAMS F.W. 65144 " EDWARDS T.F.(W/A) 52737 " HANDY E.W. (K/A) 62995 " BECKETT D. 65788 " PHILLIPS D. 77711 " GREENWOOD H.V.V. 61452 " SWABY T. 65863 " LUCK J.H. Extract from LONDON GAZETTE d/- 4/9/18 :- T/2nd Lieut. T.J.C.MUNFORD to be Temp. Lieut. 19/6/18.	App 100
WARLENCOURT EAUCOURT	21		Battn. moved off at 2.30 p.m. by march route to a tented camp at WARLENCOURT - EAUCOURT, arriving at 7.30 p.m. Lieut. H.E. MILLS joined Battn.	
	22		Major T.J.E.BLAKE awarded the D.S.O. for operations on August 9th, 16th & 21st. inst. Day spent in improving accommodation & final reorganisation preparatory to training.	
	23 24 25 26		Section & specialist training under company arrangements.	
	27		Companies carried out range practices.	

D. D. & L., London, E.C.
(A8004) Wt. W1771/M2031 750,000 5/17 Sch. 52 Forms/C2118/14

Instructions regarding War Diaries and Intelligence Summaries are contained in F. S. Regs., Part II. and the Staff Manual respectively. Title pages will be prepared in manuscript.

WAR DIARY
or
INTELLIGENCE SUMMARY.
(Erase heading not required.)

Army Form C. 2118.

Place	Date	Hour	Summary of Events and Information	Remarks and references to Appendices
WARLENCOURT EAUCOURT	27		Following decorations awarded :- Capt. T.H. WHITEHEAD, M.C. — D.S.O.) For operations on August 23rd. 2nd Lt. C.W. RANDALL. — M.C.) " H.J. Rowland. — M.C.) G10497 Sgt. FURR A.) G229693 " BUBB P.H.) G5756 L/C. DOLLIN H.) Military Medal. For operation on Sep. 4th. G46369 Pte POVEY A.E.) G61400 " MOORE H.D.) G9524 Sig. PIPPIN H.)	
	28		Battn. route march. Warning order received for Battalion to move up in relief of a battalion of 5th Division.	
	29		Order No. 219 issued. Battn. marched off at 8.30 a.m. & arrived at BEUGNY area at 11 a.m. Bn. H.Q. was at I.21.b.00.95. Another warning order received for Battn. to move further up. Verbal orders issued.	App. 101
E. of GOUZEAUCOURT	30		Battn. moved off at 9.0 a.m. & proceeded by bus to P.24.a. Dinners were served here & at 3 p.m. the Battn. marched forward to R.26. Battn. H.Q. was established at R.26.b.00.55. Strength of Battalion Off. 39 O.R's. 780.	

[illegible] Lieut. Adjt.

D. D. & L., London, E.C. (A8001) Wt. W1771/M2031 750,000 5/17 Sch. 52 Forms/C2118/14

CONFIDENTIAL

WAR DIARY

OF

13TH BN. ROYAL FUSILIERS

For Month of

OCTOBER 1918

VOLUME XXXVIII

Army Form C. 2118.

Instructions regarding War Diaries and Intelligence Summaries are contained in F. S. Regs., Part II. and the Staff Manual respectively. Title pages will be prepared in manuscript.

WAR DIARY
or
INTELLIGENCE SUMMARY.
(Erase heading not required.)

Place	Date	Hour	Summary of Events and Information	Remarks and references to Appendices
			Strength 39 Off + 780 O.R.	
N. of GONNELIEU	1/10/18		During the afternoon the Battn. was withdrawn into bivouacs along sunken road in R.25.a & c.	
			Battn. H.Q. established at R.25.b.1.7.	
N. of GOUZEAUCOURT	2/10/18		Training carried out.	
	3/10/18		Training carried out.	
	4/10/18		Training carried out. T/Capt. B. Graves, R.A.M.C. attached 13th R.Fus. awarded M.C.	
	5/10/18		Battn. was ordered to move forward into close support of the 111th Inf. Bde. Great difficulty was experienced in getting into position owing to the darkness & the lack of information received as to the location of 10th R. Fus. whose positions the Battn. were to occupy. Battn finally arrived in position as under :- No 2 Company R.30.a. & c. No 3 Company R.24.c. & M.19.a. (Sheet 57B.) No 4 " in M.14. (Sheet 57B.) No 1 Company in support about R.29.c. Battn. H.Q. at R.24.a.7.7.	
N.W. of BANTEUX	6/10/18		'A' & 'B' echelons were moved to vicinity of Battn. H.Q.	
			Nos. G7958 Pte MEBB A.H. G74820 Pte GREENSLADE J.N. No. G13786 Pte HORNER, J.H. 87268 " LAYER N.G. 79726 " HOGG A. awarded Military Medal for gallantry in action East of HAVRINCOURT, 18/9/18.	
	7/10/18		Orders for attack on GREEN LINE (HURTEBISE FARM) & road in N.15.a. N.9.c.) being objective of Battalion. C.O., & Coy. Commanders reconnoitred from BONNE ENFANCE FARM.	
			Owing to discovery of the fact that the barrage for the first objective would make it impossible for the Battn. to assemble as laid down in Brigade Orders, & the consequent	

D. D. & L., London, E.C. (A7883) Wt. W803/M1672 350,000 4/17 Sch. 52a Forms/C/2118/14

Army Form C. 2118.

Instructions regarding War Diaries and Intelligence Summaries are contained in F. S. Regs., Part II. and the Staff Manual respectively. Title pages will be prepared in manuscript.

WAR DIARY
or
INTELLIGENCE SUMMARY.
(Erase heading not required.)

Place	Date	Hour	Summary of Events and Information	Remarks and references to Appendices
			confusion ensuing; it was found too late to issue operation orders. Company Commanders received verbal instructions to assemble in the LE CATELET - NAUROY Switch, starting to cross the ESCAULT CANAL at 6.30 p.m. Battn. H.Q. moved to 13th K.R.R.C. H.Q. at M.22.b.2.1. Positions reached without difficulty.	
	8/10/18	12 M.N	C.O. conferred with C.C., 1st Essex Regt. as to alternate in assembly positions. Conference of Company Commanders called. 2nd-in-Command (Major T.H. Whitehead, DSO., M.C.) explained the attack & issued verbal instructions together with objective maps.	
			No 2 Company was ordered to move forward directly on HURTEBISE FARM (N.14.a.) while the remainder of the objective (road in N.15.c. & a. & 9.c.) was allotted to No 3 Coy. Owing to the fact that the 21st Div. on the right were not able to move up on the right in time, Nos. 1 & 4 Coys. were detailed to form defensive right rear flank from HURTEBISE FARM N.E. to LITTLE HOUSE.	
		3. A.M	Battn. assembled in M.17.a. after great difficulties, due to alteration in assembly positions the darkness of the night & a certain amount of hostile artillery fire, caused by the attack of the Corps on the right.	
		4.30 AM	Zero hour.	
		5.0 AM	Battn. moved forward towards jumping off line (RED LINE). Battn. had practically to fight its way to the jumping off line owing to the failure of the 111th Inf. Bde. to clear BEL AISE FARM (M.18.a.) & parts of the MASNIERES - BEAUREVOIR System.	
S. ?LESDAIN		6.2 AM	Battn. moved from jumping off line & advanced directly on objectives. Owing to the fact that there was still fighting going on to the S. of the first objective & also to the fact that the enemy from the high ground in N.8. & 14 were able to use their machine guns before the barrage reached them, the advance was for a time held up, about 800 yards short of the objective. Nos. 2 & 3 Coys. were able to push right on & eventually reached the GREEN LINE about 7.15 a.m. & consolidated. There was no enemy reaction; but No 2 Coy. was forced to withdraw from the Southern & Eastern sides of the farm & take up a position on the N.side for a time owing to heavy enemy fire from N.21.	[signature] Adt 13 RF

D. D. & L., London, E.C. (A7883) Wt. W1503/M1672 350,000 4/17 Sch. 52a Forms C/2118/14

Instructions regarding War Diaries and Intelligence Summaries are contained in F. S. Regs., Part II. and the Staff Manual respectively. Title pages will be prepared in manuscript.

WAR DIARY
or
INTELLIGENCE SUMMARY.
(Erase heading not required.)

Army Form C. 2118.

Place	Date	Hour	Summary of Events and Information	Remarks and references to Appendices
			The 21st Divn. did not reach the HURTEBISE FARM line until 10.30 a.m. - 3 hours after scheduled time. The 1/1st Herts Regt. passed through the Battn. to the BRISEUX WOOD line during consolidation. 13th Bn. R.Fus. H.Q. were established at N.13.d.5.9. There was very little fire after 10 a.m. & the companies rested on the objective.	
	9/10/18	3.15 A.M.	Orders to continue the advance received. Conference of Os.C.Coys. held.	
		6.0 A.M.	The Battn. moved off in support to 1/1st Herts Regt. Objective - LIGNY-en-CAMBRESIS. The leading Battalion met no opposition, & by 8 a.m. the 1/1st Herts had reached their objective, (0.3. & I.33). Artillery barrage had in the meanwhile ceased. The Battn. (Nos. 1 & 4 Coys. Right & Left Front Coys, & Nos. 2 & 3, Right & Left Support Coys respectively) moved forward on either side of LIGNY & established a line approximately of road I.33.b. & I.34.a. A certain amount of resistance was met in taking up this position from machine guns & two enemy batteries, but the line was definitely established by 10 a.m. Battn. H.Q. were established in the Chateau, LIGNY.	
		2.0 P.M.	The 1/1st Herts Regt. passed through the Battn. to attack CAUDRY, but were definitely held up by machine gun fire.	
			During the evening the Battn. received orders to establish itself on line I.33.c.0.0. - I.27.b.5.0. Later orders were issued to assemble on CLARY - LIGNY Road preparatory to moving forward at dawn to attack AUDENCOURT. This however was cancelled before the completion of the move & the Battn. eventually assembled on line I.35.a.6.8. - I.36.d.8.9. shortly before Zero (5 a.m.) Objective to form 4 strong points I.30.a. - J.19.c. - J.19.b. - J.13.b. & cut off the town of CAUDRY from the East. The 1st Essex Regt. were to carry out a similar operation on the West.	
	10/10/18	5.0 A.M.	The Battn. moved off. Practically no opposition was met. Coys. established themselves in their positions without difficulty except from the supporting tanks which persistently fired at our own troops & from our own barrage which was late & short.	

D. D. & L., London, E.C. (A7883) Wt. W809/M1672 350,000 4/17 Sch. 52a Forms C/2118/14

Instructions regarding War Diaries and Intelligence Summaries are contained in F. S. Regs., Part II. and the Staff Manual respectively. Title pages will be prepared in manuscript.

WAR DIARY
or
INTELLIGENCE SUMMARY.
(*Erase heading not required.*)

Army Form C. 2118.

Place	Date	Hour	Summary of Events and Information	Remarks and references to Appendices
			No 3 Coy. finding no opposition pushed forward across the LE CATEAU - CAMBRAI Road & captured BETHENCOURT without opposition throwing out a line of posts on the E. side of the village.	
			Lieut.Col. R.A.Smith & Major T.H. Whitehead in the meanwhile entered CAUDRY & were enthusiastically welcomed by a large number of French civilians, whom the advance of the Battalion had freed.	
		8.0AM	Battn. H.Q. established at I.30.a.6.2. Battn. reassembled. Nos. 2 & 3 Coys. in BETHENCOURT, Nos. 1 & 4 Coys, in practice trenches in J.19.b. 4th Msex Regt. in the meanwhile passing through the Battn.	
			Attached is Summary of Operations.	App 102
			Total casualties 6th - 10th inclus. 2nd Lieut. E.M.Rees (killed) 2nd Lieut. J. Kenahan (died of wounds) Capt. P.E. Lewis, 2nd Lieut.M.E.Mills, 2nd Lieut. H.J. Rowland, 2nd Lieut. J.F. Keefe, 2nd Lieut. H.Y. Daniel, 2nd Lieut. E.W. Parker, M.C. A/Capt. R.W.Cunliffe,M.C. 2nd Lieut. C.S. Jones, 2nd Lieut. J.L. Boyle, 2nd Lieut. H.G.Crosby (all wounded) & 104 O.R.	App 103
			Over 200 prisoners were captured (the majority on the 8th) & about 15 - 20 machine guns.	
BETHENCOURT	11/10/18		Battn. H.Q. moved to BETHENCOURT. Later in the day the Battn. was withdrawn & returned to CAUDRY & billeted.	
CAUDRY	12/10/18		Reorganisation.	
	13/10/18		Reorganisation & bathing.	
	14/10/18		Training. G.O.C., 112th Inf. Bde. thanked the Battn. for its good work during the past week.	
	15/10/18		Training.	

G. H. Caly[?] Lt. Col. Cmdg. 13 R.F.

D. D. & L., London, E.C. (A7853) Wt. W1073/M1672 350,000 4/17 Sch. 52a Forms C/2118/14

Instructions regarding War Diaries and Intelligence Summaries are contained in F. S. Regs., Part II. and the Staff Manual respectively. Title pages will be prepared in manuscript.

WAR DIARY
or
INTELLIGENCE SUMMARY.
(*Erase heading not required.*)

Army Form C. 2118.

Place	Date	Hour	Summary of Events and Information	Remarks and references to Appendices
	16/10/18		Training. 2nd Lieut. J. Ruse joined Battalion.	
	17/10/18		Inspection by G.O.C., 37th Divn. Genl. H.Bruce Williams addressed Battn. after inspection in which he made use of the following words : ' I am extremely pleased with the smartness of the Battn. under extremely trying conditions & also with your steadiness on parade. The work you have done under all circumstances since August 21st when the offensive opened has been of the highest order. At present you are the making of the 112th Inf. Bde. You have served under me for two years now & have never failed me or let me down. I congratulate you '	
			Lieut. (A/Capt) P.E. Lewis awarded M.C. for gallantry in action S. of HERMIES, 4/9/18.	
	18/10/18		Training & bathing.	
	19/10/18		Training & bathing.	
	20/10/18		2nd Lieut. C.H. Padwick, 2nd Lieut. A.D. Russell, 2nd Lieut. J.B. Madgson, 2nd Lieut. L.A. Foot & 2nd Lieut. T.W. Senior joined Battalion.	
	21/10/18		Training.	
	22/10/18		Battn. warned to move to VIESLY preparatory to supporting 5th Div. & 111th Inf. Bde. in attack on 23rd inst. At 12 noon order cancelled. Battn. to stand by ready to move forward to line of SELLE at 7.30 a.m. 23rd. Order No. 220 issued.	

D. D. & L., London, E.C. (A7883) Wt. W609/M1672 350,000 4/17 Sch. 52a Forms C/2118/14

Instructions regarding War Diaries and Intelligence Summaries are contained in F. S. Regs., Part II. and the Staff Manual respectively. Title pages will be prepared in manuscript.

WAR DIARY
or
INTELLIGENCE SUMMARY.
(Erase heading not required.)

Army Form C. 2118.

Place	Date	Hour	Summary of Events and Information	Remarks and references to Appendices
CAUDRY	23/10/18	0730	Battn. moved off in accordance with Order No. 220.	App 103A
BEAUDRAIN S.W. of BEAURAIN		1115	Bivouaced in Railway in E.25.	
		1315	Moved forward to E.17.a. & b. Battn. H.Q. in RED HOUSE, E.16.d.	
		2300	Moved forward via BEAURAIN - NEUVILLE to SALESCHES.	
	24/10/18	0400	Attack commenced. Account of operations in appendix. Following officer casualties : 2nd Lt. C.H. Padwick (Gas) 2nd Lt. E.L. Carter, M.M. (Killed) 2nd Lt. T.W. Senior (Missing) 2nd Lt. G.D. Hodgson (Wounded) 2nd Lt. A.H. Taylor (Wounded) 102 O.R. casualties.	App. 104
GHISSIGNIES	25/10/18	1200	Heavy shelling of GHISSIGNIES.	
		1430	Heavy shelling of GHISSIGNIES.	
		2100	Relief by 1st Essex Regt.	
		23 45	Relief complete. Nos. 1 & 4 Coys. moved to X.20.b.5.3. No 2 Coy. to FME. HERNIER, X.20.a.0[illegible] No 3 Coy. to practice trenches in X.9.a. & b. Battn. H.Q. at X.20.a.2.3.	
			The following wire was received from 112th Inf. Bde.- 'Following from 37th Div. timed 1205 hours AAA Please convey to 13th Royal Fusiliers the congratulations of the Divisional Commander on their fine work yesterday & last night AAA'	
SALESCHES	26/10/18		No 2 Company dug a defensive line to be manned in case of attack in X.14.c. & d.	
	27/10/18	1930	Battn. relieved by 4th Msex. R. & moved to billets in NEUVILLE. A letter was received from the Maire of CAUDRY thanking the Battn. for the liberation of the town on the 11th October.	

[signature] Capt. Adj. 13 R F

D. D. & L., London, E.C. (A7883) Wt. W503/M1672 350,000 4/17 Sch. 52a Forms/C2118/14

Instructions regarding War Diaries and Intelligence Summaries are contained in F. S. Regs., Part II. and the Staff Manual respectively. Title pages will be prepared in manuscript.

WAR DIARY
or
INTELLIGENCE SUMMARY.
(Erase heading not required.)

Army Form C. 2118.

Place	Date	Hour	Summary of Events and Information	Remarks and references to Appendices
NEUVILLE	28/10/18	1830	Battn. moved to BEAURAIN to billets & bivouacs.	
BEAURAIN	29/10/18		Reorganisation. Lieut-Col. R.A. Smith, D.S.O.,M.C. went on leave. Command taken over by Major T.H. Whitehead, D.S.O.,M.C.	
	30/10/18		Reorganisation & training.	
	31/10/18		Training.	
			Strength :- 32 Officers & 604 Other Ranks.	

[signature] Capt. Adjt. 13 R.F.

D. D. & L., London, E.C.
(A7883) Wt. W809/M1672 350,000 4/17 Sch. 52a Forms/C/2118/14

S U M M A R Y   of   O P E R A T I O N S

carried out by 13th Bn. R O Y A L   F U S I L I E R S

7th to 11th OCTOBER, 1918.

Reference SHEETS - 57B.N.W., S.W., & N.E., 1/20,000.

On 7th October the battalion was lying in old German trenches along the W. bank of the ESCAUT Canal between BANTEUX and VAUCELLES, with Battalion H.Q. at R.24.a.7.7.

On 7th October the battalion received orders to attack & capture the line HURTEBISE FARM (inclusive) and line of sunken road, N.15.c.0.3. - N.9.c.7.1. (Div. second objective, known as the GREEN LINE).
The 1st Essex Regt. would attack in conjunction on the left & capture & consolidate sunken road in N.9.central.
Inter-battalion boundary line M.23.a.00.55. - N.9.c.1.7.
Preliminary reconnaissances were made by C.O. and Company Commanders from BONNE ESPERANCE FARM on the afternoon of 7th inst. Before returning the C.O. conferred with O.C., 13th K.R.R.C. whose battalion was the Right Battalion of the 111th Inf. Bde. detailed for the first objective (RED LINE) with a view to arranging a passage through the 13th K.R.R.C. on to the forming up line in sunken road, N.7. & 13.central. It was then discovered that the barrage for the 111th Inf. Bde. attack would make it impossible for the 13th R.Fus. to reach their forming up line in N.7. & 13. by Zero plus 92 minutes, the time for starting off for the second objective, unless they moved through the barrage for the 111th Inf. Bde. The consent of 112th Inf. Bde. to form up in N.17. was obtained.

The battalion moved up into resting positions into the CATELET NAUROY LINE, arriving about 11.0 p.m. Battalion H.Q. was established by H.Q. of K.R.R.C. at M.22.d.8.4.

C.O., 13th R.Fus. got into touch with O.C., 1st Essex Regt. & arranged with him that the battalion should be able to form up in M.17.c. Great difficulty was experienced in forming up owing to the darkness of the night & to the fact that there were very few natural features to assist platoon and company commanders in finding their positions. The battalion, however, was assembled ready to move off by Zero hour - 4.30 a.m.
From 1 to 4.0 a.m. there was a certain amount of hostile artillery fire due to the attack of the Corps on the right. This, however, did not interfere very much with assembly.

At Zero plus 30 -(5.0 a.m.)- the battalion moved forward to reach jumping off line FOR second objective. A lot of opposition was met with in M.18.b. as left battalion of the 111th Inf. Bde. had not succeeded in mopping up BEL AISE FARM. The jumping off line was however reached by Zero plus 92, at which hour barrage lifted. The battalion advanced, with No 2 Coy. on the right, No 3 Coy. on the left, straight towards their objective, namely, HURTEBISE FARM -(No 2 Coy.), remainder of objective -(No 3 Coy.) Nos. 1 and 4 Coys. were ordered to form a defensive right flank on line from M.18.b.3.4. to HURTEBISE FARM, where they were again in touch with No 2 Coy. The 2 leading companies met with considerable opposition, coming under very heavy machine gun fire from MEZIERES COPSE, HURTEBISE FARM & strong point in N.14.a.7.4. Enemy troops holding HURTEBISE FARM were able to get their machine guns into action at 800 yards, firing through the barrage & causing considerable casualties to the advancing companies. In consequence the advance was hung up about 600 yds. off the objective & the front line lost the advantage of the barrage. As the barrage passed over the farm, enemy machine guns were for the time being silenced, which enabled the companies to move forward another 100 yds. The last 500 yds. however, were crossed without the assistance of artillery, sections and platoons giving each other mutual support with rifle & Lewis gun fire. Valuable assistance was also given by 4 machine guns of 'C' Coy. 37th Machine Gun Battn. who were attached to the battalion. This section was able to obtain direct fire on the enemy, doing considerable execution.

No 2 Company reached HURTEBISE FARM about Zero plus 180, i.e. 7.30 a.m. where many prisoners and machine guns were taken. A line was consolidated on S. edge of the farm. 13 R.F.
The 21st Divn. who were due to arrive at the same time as ours did not appear until 10.30 a.m. up to which time No 2 Coy. had some trouble with hostile minenwerfers & machine guns from N.21.a. & b.
In the meantime, Left Coy - No 3 - had reached the line N.14.b.0.0. - N.14.b.0.7. when enemy who had been hiding in a dug-out at N.14.a.7.4. came out & opened machine gun fire on them from the rear. Great trouble was experienced with this pocket & it was not until the arrival of a tank that it could be finally dealt with. 2 enemy officers were killed on the machine guns & 18 prisoners captured. The line then went forward & took up their final objective. Battn. H.Q. was established at N.13.c.5.9.

200 prisoners & about a dozen machine guns were captured by the battalion during this operation.

After the 1/1st Herts Regt. had passed through into BRISEUX WOOD, organisation was completed.

Orders that the advance would be resumed on the 9th were received on the early morning of that day.

Brigade would pass through the 63rd Inf. Bde. on the first objective, 13th R.Fus. was ordered to pass through 1/1st Herts Regt. on the GREEN LINE immediately W. of LIGNY-en-CAMBRESIS with the 1st Essex Regt. on their left, at 11.20 a.m. & consolidate the line O.5.a.0.3. - I.35.a.6.3. - I.27.d.6.0.
No opposition was met with by the leading brigades & battalions. Battalion passed through 1/1st Herts W. of LIGNY about 8.0 a.m. Very little opposition was met with & the battalion consolidated on its objective in touch with the 17th Division at I.34.b.9.2. & with 1st Essex Regt. at I.34.a.2.9.
About 20 prisoners were taken in LIGNY while mopping up.
1/1st Herts Regt. passed through battalion at 2.0 p.m. to take CAUDRY, but practically no progress was made. Orders were issued about 7.0 p.m. to take up line I.35.c.0.0. - I.27.b.5.0. (inclusive)
Companies arrived in new position about 9.0 p.m. Battalion was ordered to assemble in J.32.c. & d. & to take AUDENCOURT, making a strong point there & J.14.c. with the object of cutting off CAUDRY from the East. This was to be carried out subsequent to the capture of the railway line in J.32. & 33. by the Division on the right.
Companies moved into assembly positions at LIGNY - CLARY Road.
Orders were later received cancelling the attack on AUDENCOURT & fresh orders were issued to ~~take~~ attack N. of CAUDRY, making 4 strong points at I.30.a. - J.19.c. - J.19.b. - J.13.b. with the object of cutting CAUDRY off from the East.
Position of assembly I.35.a.6.8. I.36.d.8.9. Companies formed up :-
No 1 Coy. on the right, No 2 Coy. on the left, No 4 Coy. left support, No 3 Coy. right support.......................................
at Zero hour - 5.0 a.m. - 17th Division operating on the right, crossing the railway at 5.20 a.m.
Companies moved off under barrage & crossed the railway in I.30.c. & d. at 5.20 a.m.
No opposition was met with at first, but movement could not be rapid owing to the numbers of isolated houses. Two tanks which were moving in support to the battalion in I.29.c. lost direction & opened fire with their 6 pdrs. on the advancing Coys. It was with great difficulty that they were prevailed upon to cease fire. Also 2 - 18 pdr. guns firing barage were shooting about 1200 yards short.
Objectives were reached with ~~very little~~ no opposition ~~from~~ except from a few enemy riflemen.
Two low flying enemy aeroplanes also attacked battalion, but were driven off by the concentrated fire of every rifle & Lewis Gun of the battalion.
On arrival at objective, J.14.c. the leading company - No 3 - decided to move forward & by so doing was able to occupy BETHENCOURT & throw out an outpost line at Eastern edge of the village in J.8.c. & d.
Patrols were at once pushed out into CAUDRY & by 6.0 a.m. the whole town had been covered with few enemy remaining in it being captured.
C.O. at once obtained an interview with the Maire, with whom arrangements were made for the prohibition of giving alcohol to the troops, & steps taken for prevention of looting.

Large crowds of civilians collected, who welcomed the battalion with enth

At 8.0 a.m. the whole battalion was withdrawn from the village. 2 comp occupied BETHENCOURT, other 2 companies in practice trenches in J.19.b. Batt H.Q. was established at I.30.a.6.2.

Total casualties for the operations 8th, 9th & 10th :-

13 Officers
and
102 Other Ranks.

Guy R. Chapman
Capt & Adjt.
18 R.F.
15.10.18

SECRET.
Copy No.........

13th Bn. ROYAL FUSILIERS.

ORDER NO. 221.

22/10/18.

Ref. SHEET - 57B. N.W. 1/20,000.
57B. N.E. "
51A. S.E. "

---

1. The advance will be continued to-morrow, 23rd.
Maps showing objectives, etc., will be issued to O.C. Coys. on parade to-morrow, 23rd.

2. The 112th Inf. Bde. (less 1st Essex Regt.) is detailed in support to 111th Inf. Bde.

(a) It will move forward into position of readiness on Railway E. of BRIASTRE by 11.00 hours, 23rd inst.

(b) Battn. will occupy positions as under :-

No 1 Coy. K.1.b. E. of road.
4 " E.25.d. "
2 " K.1.a. & b. between road & railway.
3 " E.25.c. & d. " " "

3. Battn. will parade in column of fours facing N. in the Rue de GAMBETTA at 07.30 hours. Starting Point will be street corner I.34.a.4.4.
Order of Companies :- H.Q.
No 4 Coy. with Lewis gun limber.
2 " " " " "
3 " " " " "
1 " " " " "

Head of the column will pass Starting Point at 07.30 hours.
200 yards distance will be observed between Coys. W. of BETHENCOURT.
150 " " " " " " Platoons E. of BETHENCOURT.

ROUTE will be BETHENCOURT - VIESLY - D.29.c.3.1. J.6.a.1.2. D.30.d.45.40

4. SELLE R. will be crossed by footbridges in E.25.c. There is one footbridge to each 100 yards.
Lewis gun limbers will be unloaded at D.30.d.45.40.

5. MEN & EQUIPMENT.- Fighting Order. Packs will be carried.

(a) Blankets & overcoats rolled in bundles of 10, also haversacks, will be dumped at Q.M's stores by 06.45 hours.
Men will carry cooked food for 23rd inst.

(b) Officers' kits & mess boxes, etc., will be at Q.M's stores by 07.00 hrs.

6. TRANSPORT.- (a) Each Company will be accompanied by its Lewis gun limber. T.O. will detail one limber to report to Battn. H.Q. at 06.30 hours. This limber will be used for Lewis gun & signal equipment.

(b) Travelling kitchens of Nos. 2 & 4 Coys. will accompany the column together with one water cart. On arrival at D.30.d.45.40 they will proceed via BRIASTRE & report to Battn. H.Q.

7. Reports will be sent to head of the column until SELLE R. is crossed. Battn. H.Q. will then be established as near as possible to cross roads at E.25.b.0.2.

8. FIGHTING EQUIPMENT.- R.S.M. will arrange for each Coy. limber to carry 3000 rounds bandolier packed S.A.A. This will be taken from Coy. limbers on off-loading & issued at the railway & on the scale of one bandolier per O.R.

P.T.O.

Capt. & Adjutant.
13th R. Fus.

ISSUED at.....11.20.........

Copy No 1 to C.O.
2 No 1 Coy.
3 2 "
4 3 "
5 4 "
6 H.Q.Coy.
7 Q.M.
8 T.O.
9 R.S.M.
10 & 11 War Diary.
12 File.

13th Bn. R O Y A L F U S I L I E R S.

App 104

OPERATIONS 23rd - 25th October, 1918.

Ref. Sheets : 57B. N.E. 1/20,000 Squares J.D.E.K.F.
51A. S.E. 1/20,000 Squares W.X.R.

Date.	Hour.	
22.10.18	23.15	Brigade Order No. 240 received. Battn. Order No. 220 issued. Battn. remained in billets at CAUDRY.
23.10.18	07.30	Battn. with 'A' Echelon, moved from CAUDRY via PETIT CAUDRY - BETHENCOURT to VIESLY. - where congestion in traffic necessitated a detour across country from the road laid down. Crossed SELLE R.
	11.15	(at E.25.c.1.8.) & got into assembly position on Railway in E.25.d. & K.1.b. Battn. bivouaced. Dinners eaten.
	12.50	Orders received to move forward behind 111th Inf. Bde. at 13.00 hrs & occupy squares E.17.a. & c.
	13.15 15.00	Battn. moved off & took up positions indicated. Battn. H.Q. at RED HOUSE, E.16.d.
	19.30	Conference of Brigade Commander with Os.C. 13th R.F., 1/1st Herts, C.Coy. M.G. Battn. & 112 T.M.B.

Verbal instructions for operations from DOTTED GREEN LINE (reported held by 111th Inf. Bde.) at 04.00 hours, 24th.

OBJECTIVE - Line of sunken road from R.34.a.5.2. to road & Railway junct. X.5.a.2.9.

LINE of EXPLOITATION - Eastwards to line of RAILWAY R.35.a. & c.
N.Z. Divn. on left, 1/1st Herts R. on right, 1st Essex R. in support.
Right flank E. of SALESCHES - LE QUESNOY Railway known to be exposed.

Light barrage (100 yds. in 3 minutes) would accompany Battn. gradually thinning out & ceasing before arrival at GHISSIGNIES.

Battn. to commence approach march at 23.00 hrs. in rear of 1/1st Herts R.

	21.00	Conference of Os.C.Coys. held at the RED HOUSE.

Frontages allotted :-

No 1 Coy.	....	Right Front.
2 "	....	" Support.
3 "	....	Left Front.
4 "	....	" Support.

	22.00	C.O. went forward to Bde. H.Q. in BEAURAIN for further & amended instructions. Road X.15. X.10 dividing line between Battns.
	23.00	Battn. moved off in order :-

No 4 Company.
1 "
3 "
2 "

Heavy congestion of traffic in BEAURAIN. Battn. hung up here until mid-night.

24.10.18	00.01	Major T.H. Whitehead, D.S.O.,M.C. led Battn. Route via ST. MAURICE CHAPEL - NEUVILLE. Progress extremely difficult owing to congestion in traffic.

24.10.18. 00.01 A certain amount of H.E. & Blue Cross shelling.

Battn. halted in NEUVILLE & awaited orders.

03.00 Battn. moved forward through SALESCHES to assembly position. Battn. H.Q. at W.24.d.0.1.

It was reported by N.Z. Divn. that they held approx. lines X20.b.8.8. - X.9.d.0.5. - X.2.d.8.5.
Arty. barrage altered to clear the line, but would remain on practice trenches in X.9.

03.45 Coys. in assembly position on GREEN DOTTED LINE from X.20.b.60.45 - X.14.c.3.5. There was some shelling at this point, especially of No 2 Coy. (Right Support) during which the Company Commander, 2nd Lieut. E.L. Carter, M.M. was killed.

Os.C. Nos. 1 & 4 Coys. went forward to reconnoitre line of advance. A strong belt of wire (previously unreported) was found in front of BROWN LINE.

04.00 Battn. moved forward under barrage. A certain amount of bunching was necessary owing to wire. This was however crossed successfully without losing the barrage. Machine gun fire was encountered from the right, 135 contour in X.21.b. No 1 Coy. at this time finding that the 1/1st Herts R. were not coming forward on the right, swung ~~[illegible]~~ outwards.
(Right Support) No 2 Coy's leading platoons with which the two rear platoons had lost touch, were held up by ~~hedges~~ hedges. On reforming on the far side, direction was lost. These two platoons eventually ~~coming~~ came up on the right of No 1 Coy. E. of the SALESCHES - GHISSIGNIES Road & filled up a gap with No 3 Coy. 1/1st Herts R. who had by this time come up. The advance was then continued.

Left Coy. (No 4 Coy) moved off behind barrage, & though experiencing difficulty in crossing the barbed wire in front of the BROWN LINE, did not lose the assistance of the artillery. This was probably due to the barrage being slightly slower than the pace of the attacking troops, who were twice halted to avoid being shelled by our own guns. At the same time Major Whitehead finding that the 1/1st Herts R. were not advancing, ordered No 3 Coy. (Left Support) & the remaining two platoons of No 2 Coy. to swing right & form a defensive flank against the enemy who were still holding the high ground in X.21.b. No 3 Coy. immediately occupied a position in X.15.c. slightly W. of the road. with the two platoons of No 2 Coy. slightly further north.

05.30 Leading Coys. crossed the approximate grid line E. & W. through X.9.central. Here a certain amount of opposition was met & eventually after a sharp fighting about 50 prisoners were taken in X.9.b.
During this period all Coys. were under machine gun fire from X.10.c. X.5. & X.11.
Left Coy. (No 4) was also held up by new wire in X.9.

07.00 The advance had been resumed. No 4 Coy. crossed the river, the left 2 platoons wading about X.3.b.8.0. right 2 platoons crossing by bridge at X.4.c.6.7.
The right company crossed by bridge at X.4.d.0.4. shortly followed by the 2 leading platoons of No 2 Coy.
Some further 50 prisoners were taken before the ECAILLON was crossed.

crossed.

The 1/1st Herts had by this time come up & were forming a defensive right flank in X.10.c.

After crossing ENAILLON, 2 platoons of No 4 Coy. attempted to push forward up road in X.4.a.8.0. - R.34.d.8.2. but were definitely hung up by machine gun fire from front & flank about the road bend X.4.b.2.7. Enemy aeroplanes were also extremely active with M.G. fire against this Coy.
The left 2 platoons of the same Coy. were also hung up about the line of the road at X.3.b.9.7. & X.4.a.2.2.
No 1 Coy. on right, pushed up road X.4.d.7.2. - CHAPEL in X.5.
Here they were met by very heavy fire from the CHAPEL & also from right flank, the leading platoon being practically wiped out to a man.
At the same time a platoon of No 2 Coy. & a platoon of the 1/1st Herts R. who were in the village, were pushed forward by O.C., No 1 Coy. & placed in copse X.4.b. X.5.a.
A reconnoitring patrol of No 2 Coy. also pushed Eastwards as far as X.5.c.9.3. without encountering enemy. About 20 - 30 more prisoners were also cleaned up in GHISSIGNIES.

08.00 (Left Coy) Position was approximately as attached tracing 'A'.
At this time O.C., No 4 Coy. realising that he could not reach his objective by pushing up the road X.4.a.8.0. R.34.d.8.2. & that he was losing men all the time, resolved to withdraw his two platoons on the road. Having done this he moved the whole of his Coy. Westwards & eventually reaching a position about R.34.c.2.7. moved N.E. & occupied sunken road in R.34.c. (objective) Pushing forward, the company by now reduced to under 40 strong, occupied & consolidated a small orchard about 200 yds. forward of the road. Touch was shortly afterwards found with the N.Z. Div. on the left, but touch on the right was definitely lost.

During this period O.C. No 1 Coy. having touch on neither flank, & finding he was losing men very quickly, decided to withdraw. The platoon of No 2 Coy. was withdrawn from the copse in X.4.b. X.5.a. (platoon of 1/1st Herts having already gone back) & together with the remainder of No 1 Coy. an outpost line was thrown out along hedges in X.4.b. & d. with a main line in front of the Northern edge of GHISSIGNIES. A defensive flank was also formed between the river & the cross roads X.4.d.7.2.

09.45 Position was as attached tracing (B).
No 3 Coy. had moved up in the meantime via X.3.d. & SAINT ROCH & was occupying hedges about R.34.c.4.2. X.4.a.8.8. X.4.a.2.6. with one platoon in reserve in sunken road X.4.c.6.8. Touch could not be gained with No 4 Coy.
The position remained substantially the same throughout the day.
There was spasmodic shelling of GHISSIGNIES.

18.00 Touch after several unsuccessful attempts was eventually established with Left Coy. (No 4) whose right at the time was completely exposed.
Orders were received to secure the objective in conjunction with 1/1st Herts R. at 9.0 p.m. under a short 2 minutes barrage. & that the Battn. would be relieved by 1st Essex R. on completion of operations.
One platoon (No 9) of Left Support (No 3 Coy) was detailed for this operation.
Platoon was given orders to capture cross roads R.34.d.8.2. & sunken road N.W.

20.45 Platoon formed up about hedge in R.34.c.0.0. & advanced.

	21.00	Platoon from about 100 yds. short of objective, rushed in under the barrage & occupied cross roads. Moving N.W. up road they captured a machine gun & gained touch with the right of No 4 Coy. 1/1st Herts did not gain the objective.
25.10.18.	04.00	Relief by 1st Essex R. cancelled. During the day the enemy at 12.00 & 14.30 hours put down heavy barrages on GHISSIGNIES. O.C., No 4 Coy. while attempting to get forward with the N.Z. Div. near Fme. DE LA BEART was wounded.
	21.00	Relief by 1st Essex R. commenced. Battn. withdrew to trenches in X.9. & to barns & cellars in SALESCHES.

<u>Casualties</u> 23rd - 25/10/18 :-

6 Off. 102 O.R.

<u>Strength</u> on 25/10/18 :-

11 Off. & 269 O.R.

About 120 prisoners were taken, together with numerous machine guns.
One 150 mm. gun & one 210 mm. 7 T.M's & 30 machine guns were captured
About 15 civilians were found in the same village.

G. H. Chapman
Capt & Adjt
13 R.F.

28/10/18

13th Bn. ROYAL FUSILIERS.

N O T E S on the attacks, 24/10/18.

1. HEDGES.- Great difficulty was experienced both in assembly & during the advance owing to the thickness of hedges. In several cases by going round, platoons lost direction. Also during the attack on the evening of the 24th, the attack could not have been made frontally owing to the impossibility of getting through the hedges.

It is recommended that a certain number of bill hooks (8 per Coy.) be issued from Brigade mobile reserve or from Pioneer Battn. prior to an attack during an advance through country of the present enclosed nature.

In addition to above, every man should have a Cutter wire swallow tail attached to his rifle.

2. WIRE CUTTERS.- Wirecutters have proved themselves absolutely necessary in enclosed country. Practically every hedge is wired by civilians in order to strengthen it.

It is recommended that every man's rifle be equipped with a pair of swallow tail wirecutters. The Mk. V wirecutter is too cumbersome & is easily lost.

3. Time keeping 'T.M.' - This was found extremely useful on the night of 24th, & should always prove valuable in minor operations.

WAR DIARY

OF

13TH BN. ROYAL FUSILIERS

FOR MONTH OF

NOVEMBER 1918

VOLUME 39

Instructions regarding War Diaries and Intelligence Summaries are contained in F. S. Regs., Part II, and the Staff Manual respectively. Title pages will be prepared in manuscript.

WAR DIARY
or
INTELLIGENCE SUMMARY.
(Erase heading not required.)

Army Form C. 2118.

Place	Date	Hour	Summary of Events and Information	Remarks and references to Appendices
BEAURAIN	1/11/18		Strength of Battalion 31 Officers 607 Other Ranks. Battn. warned for attack on FORET DE MORMAL. Training. H.V. guns shelled BEAURAIN. Owing to extreme weakness of battalion since the operations of 24th Oct. Battn. was reorganised on a two company basis - 'A' & 'B' Coys. - under command of Capt. G.G. Ziegler & Capt. M.C. Lewis respectively. Coys. about 100 strong each on new organisation.	
			The Corps Commander, under authority granted by His Majesty the King, awarded the following decorations to the u/m O.R.- for gallantry & devotion to duty nr. HURTEBISE FARM (S.of ESNES) 8/10/18 :- THE MILITARY MEDAL. 53266 L/Cpl. (A/Cpl) H.H. Scull. 225870 Sgt. J.W. Stringer. 42340 Cpl. L. Green. 65857 Pte (L/Cpl) W. Shuttlewood. 52053 Pte C.H. Pym. 87564 Pte F.C.Hicks. 65164 " A.J. Smith. 65693 L/Cpl. G.A. Collis. 42550 L/C.W.H.Mason. 228838 L/C. J.H. Beardsley. 50970 Pte J. Wareham. (Authy : Corps No. A56/33 d/- 30/10/18)	
	2/11/18		Conference with O.C., 1st Essex Regt. & O.C., 8th Som. L.I. Previous experience of enclosed ground at GHISSIGNIES on 24th Oct. enabled adequate preparation in the way of wirecutters, bill hooks & hand axes to be made. Enemy H.V. guns shelled BEAURAIN.	
	3/11/18	10.15	Order No. 222 issued.	APP 105
		12.45	Order No. 223 issued. Conference of Company Commanders.	APP 106
		15.10	Order No. 224 issued. This was necessitated by heavy counter preparation by enemy on trenches in X.9.a. & b. on night 2/3rd.	APP 107
BALESCHES		17.40	Coys. moved from BEAURAIN in accordance with Order No. 224. On arrival at FME. BERNIER. tents were pitched & companies were under cover by 20.30 hrs.	
GHISSIGNIES FME. DE L'HOPITAL	4/11/18	06.45 08.00 11.30	After breakfasts had been eaten, Battn. moved forward in support to 1st Essex Regt. Account of operations is given in appendix.	APP 108

G.G. [signature] Capt. + Adjt.
13 R.F.

D. D. & L., London, E.C.
(A7883) Wt. W803/M1672 350,000 4/17 Sch. 52a Forms/C/2118/14

Instructions regarding War Diaries and Intelligence Summaries are contained in F. S. Regs., Part II. and the Staff Manual respectively. Title pages will be prepared in manuscript.

WAR DIARY
or
INTELLIGENCE SUMMARY.
(Erase heading not required.)

Army Form C. 2118.

Place	Date	Hour	Summary of Events and Information	Remarks and references to Appendices
JOLIMETZ	4/11/18	13.00	Great praise is due to the N.C.O. commanding No. 9 platoon, No. 8021 Sgt. GREEN W. who with	
ROND QUESNE		16.00	great daring pushed his platoon right through the FORET DE MORMAL in complete darkness, arriving on the **final** objective at 18.30 hours.	
			No other platoons were able to come up with him during the night. However he & his platoon remained on the objective & patrolled the ground for about 1000 yards Eastwards until morning, when the 5th Division passed through.	
			Praise must also be given to the Battn. H.Q. signallers & **runners**. The former laid during the day some 6000 yards of **cable** & maintained lines with the greatest diligence, both to Coys. & to Brigade, although extremely short handed. Scarcely one of the runners can have walked less than 20 miles during the day, & several ver much more. It is entirely due to these two bodies of men that communications were easily kept in very difficult country, & that the usual difficulties attendant on a long & rapid advance were overcome.	
ROND QUESNE	5/11/18	09.00	Battn. withdrew to ROND QUESNE after the 5th Division had passed through & breakfasted.	
LOUVIGNIES		11.15	Battn. moved to LOUVIGNIES & billeted. Lieut. G.A. Gillman joined Battn.	
	6/11/18		Draft of 121 O.R. joined Battn. 4 company organisation was resumed.	
			2nd Lieuts. S.D. Gibbins & H. Einstein joined Battn.	
	7/11/18		Battn. bathing & reorganizing.	
	8/11/18		Work on clearing the battlefield in S.6. & 12. FORET DE MORMAL.	
	9/11/18		Training.	
	10/11/18		Order No. 225 issued.	APP. 109
BETHENCOURT	11/11/18		Battn. found Guard of Honour for Prince YORAHITO at BERTINCOURT. Battn. moved to BETHENCOURT in accordance with Order No.225. Armistice took effect from 11.00 hours.	

[illegible signature] Capt. Adjt. 13 R.F.

D. D. & L., London, E.C. (A7883) Wt. W809/M1672 350,000 4/17 Sch. 52a Forms/C/2118/14

Instructions regarding War Diaries and Intelligence Summaries are contained in F. S. Regs., Part II. and the Staff Manual respectively. Title pages will be prepared in manuscript.

WAR DIARY
or
INTELLIGENCE SUMMARY.
(Erase heading not required.)

Army Form C. 2118.

Place	Date	Hour	Summary of Events and Information	Remarks and references to Appendices
BETHENCOURT			Bodies of dead killed on 24/10/18 were buried at CHISSIGNIES. It was found that the majority of the men had been deliberately shot through the head by the enemy. The men in question had been wounded ; those that were able to walk were taken by the enemy & the remainder dealt with as stated above. Bodies of men of the Lincolnshire Regt. who had been killed about 30th Oct. were found to have been mutilated, hands hacked off at the wrists & eyes gorged out.	
	12/11/18		Reorganisation.	
	13/11/18		Presentation of medal ribands by G.O.C., IV Corps at CAUDRY.	
			Preparations for move Eastwards began.	
	14/11/18		Reorganisation. Following officers of Msex. Regt. joined battalion :- Lieut. H.P.Burton, Lieut. J.A. Cowper, 2nd Lieut. H.J. Beresford, 2nd Lieut. J.T. Hiney & A.F. Munn.	
	15/11/18		Training. Brigade Transport Competition. Battn. won 2 events out of five.	
	16/11/18		Route march.	
	17/11/18		Major T.H. Whitehead,D.S.O.,M.C. assumed command of Battn. vice Lieut-Col. R.A.Smith, D.S.O., M.C. commanding 112th Inf. Bde. during absence on leave of Brig.Genl. W.N. Herbert.	
	18/11/18		Ceremonial parade. The following decoration was awarded (London Gazette 30/10/18) **DISTINGUISHED CONDUCT MEDAL.** No G/7778 Pte (A/L/Cpl.) BUTLER W. No 2 Coy. for conspicuous gallantry near BUCQUOY during an enemy raid 12/7/18.	

[signature] Lt. Col. 13 RF

D. D. & L., London, E.C. (A7853) Wt. W807/M1672 350,000 4/17 Sch. 52a Forms C/2118/14

Instructions regarding War Diaries and Intelligence Summaries are contained in F. S. Regs., Part II. and the Staff Manual respectively. Title pages will be prepared in manuscript.

WAR DIARY
or
INTELLIGENCE SUMMARY.
(Erase heading not required.)

Army Form C. 2118.

Place	Date	Hour	Summary of Events and Information	Remarks and references to Appendices
BETHENCOURT	19/11/18		Following decorations were awarded by G.O.C., IV Corps, for gallantry & devotion to duty near GHISSIGNIES on 24th Oct. 1918 :- BAR to MILITARY MEDAL. No. 53266 Cpl. H.H. Boull, M.M. No 1 Coy. 226109 Pte T.H. Bennett, M.M. 1 " 225370 Sgt. J.W. Stringer, M.M. 2 " 65786 Pte D. Phillips, M.M. 4 " MILITARY MEDAL. 12260 Sgt. A.J. Elsey No 1 Coy. 87487 Pte H.J. Smith 1 " 5836 " W. Earl 1 " (Transport. 27831 " L. Akehurst 2 " 79741 L/C. E. Ridley 4 " 11173 Cpl. J. Banks No 1 Coy. 79724 L/Cpl. A.B. Hill 1 " 42193 L/Cpl. H.H. Baker No 2 Coy. 225278 Sgt. (A/CSM) F.H. Goble, No 4 Coy	
			Practice Brigade Ceremonial parade for Divisional Commander's inspection.	
	20/11/18		Practice Brigade Ceremonial parade.	
	21/11/18		Brigade Ceremonial Parade for G.O.C., 37th Divn.	
			Lieut. W.P. Trotter, M.C. joined Battalion.	
	22/11/18		The G.O.C., 37th Div. inspected the Division at CAUDRY.	
	24/11/18		Lieut. R.W. Brothers (4th R.W.Kent Rgt.) joined Battn.	
	25/11/18		The Military Medal was awarded to the u/m for gallantry in action near the FORET DE MORMAL 4/11/18.- No.G/5920 Pte Mayer E. No 2 Coy. (Bn.H.Q.) 75214 Pte Smith P. No 4 Coy. (Bn.H.Q.) 4749 Sig. Barton F. No 2 Coy. (Bn.H.Q.) Lieut. (A/Capt) S.H. Adler joined Battn. Battn. on Brigade Route march.	

A6945 Wt. W11422/M1160 350,000 12/16 D. D. & L. Forms/C./2118/14.

Army Form C. 2118.

WAR DIARY
or
INTELLIGENCE SUMMARY.
(Erase heading not required.)

Instructions regarding War Diaries and Intelligence Summaries are contained in F. S. Regs., Part II. and the Staff Manual respectively. Title pages will be prepared in manuscript.

Place	Date	Hour	Summary of Events and Information	Remarks and references to Appendices
BETHENCOURT	26/18		Without incident.	
	29/11/18		Order No. 226 issued.	APP 110
	30/11/18		Capt. E. Lander, Lieut. F.R. Mills, 2nd Lieuts. A.J. West, P. Hampshire & A.H.Starling joined battalion.	
			Strength of battalion : 32 officers 590 other Ranks.	

(A7092). Wt. W12839/M1293. 750,000. 1/17. D. D. & L., Ltd. Forms/C.2118/14.

NOTES ON THE OPERATIONS 4th & 5th November, 1918.

1. TOUCH & FRONTAGE.- It was found quite impossible to maintain constant touch on the flanks & even between companies during the whole operation. This was due (a) to the enclosed nature of the country (b) to the extreme weakness of the Battalion.
The Battalion was covering a frontage of 1000 yards, with 2 Coys. each approximately 100 strong. This necessitated a platoon covering a frontage of 250, i.e. about 12 - 14 yards per man. There is no doubt that had any serious resistance been made by the enemy it would have been quite impossible to reach the final objective.

It is suggested that at least one man to every 5 yards is a sine qua non in operations in enclosed country such as the FORET de MORMAL.

2. PACK ANIMALS.- Pack animals for carriage of Lewis gun magazines & signal apparatus were invaluable & could have been used the whole way up to the RED LINE.

3. SIGNAL SERVICES.- (a) The only means of communication owing to the nature of the country were telephone & runners. Insufficient cable was forthcoming until late in the afternoon of 4th. Battn. had by this time used up all their wire. It is suggested that a wagon load of cable be sent forward to definite points at definite times, where units may draw. The wagon should keep up very close to the rear waves of the advancing infantry. As the basis for communications forward of the enemy front line is usually line laid by Battn. signallers, it is suggested that the Signal services R.E. should provide Battalion with necessary transport for cable.

(b) It was impossible to speak to Brigade for nearly two hours on the morning of 5th inst. It is understood that this was partly due to Brigade Signals refusing to take calls & partly owing to the line being broken.

It is submitted that the Brigade Signal Section repeatedly fails in its duties towards Battalion.

4. MEDICAL SERVICES.- Car loading posts do not get forward quickly enough. At 18.00 hours, 4th. the nearest car loading post was in LOUVIGNIES (6000 yards from the front line). There were no bearer relay posts & no wheeled stretchers. Consequently one party of bearers had to carry from R.A.P. in ROND QUESNOY to LOUVIGNIES without any relay.

It is submitted that R.A.M.C. Operation Orders should state where it is intended to establish [relay] posts & car loading posts & at what times, in order to assist M.O's attached Battalions.

---oOo---

Capt. & Adjt.
for O.C., 13th Bn. ROYAL FUSILIERS.

8/11/18.

APP. 109

COPY NO. 10

13th Bn. ROYAL FUSILIERS.

ORDER NO. 225.

10/11/18.

Ref. Sheet 51.A. 1/40,000
57.B. "

---

1. The Battalion will move to BETHENCOURT to-morrow, 11th inst. & billet there.
   ROUTE : SALESCHES - NEUVILLE - BEAURAIN - MAROU - BELLEVUE - BRIASTRE - VIESLY.

2. (a) Starting point will be Road Junction X.12.a.65.90 (LOUVIGNIES CHURCH).

   (b) Coys. will ~~xxx~~ pass starting point in following order :-

   Band
   H.Q. Coy.
   No 4 Coy.
   3 "
   2 "
   1 "
   Police
   Transport

   Leading Coy. will pass starting point at 09.50 hours.

3. DRESS : Marching Order.

4. (a) Reveille will be at 07.00 hours.
   Breakfasts 08.00 hours.
   Sick Parade 08.30 hours.

   (b) Haversack rations will be carried on the march. Tea will be served at the long halt. Dinners will be eaten on arrival in billets.

   (c) Blankets rolled in bundles of 10, officers' kits, mess boxes, etc., will be loaded at Q.M's stores at 08.45 hours.

5. Travelling kitchens will move in rear of companies.
   Q.M. will make arrangements for meals in accordance with above.

------00000------

ISSUED at 23.00

Capt. & Adjutant,
13th Bn. ROYAL FUSILIERS.

Copy No 1 to C.O.
2 No 1 Coy.
3 2 "
4 3 "
5 4 "
6 H.Q. "
7 R.S.M.
8 Q.M.
9 T.O.
10 & 11 War Diary.
12 File.

App 110

SECRET.
COPY No...11...

13th Bn. ROYAL FUSILIERS. ORDER No. 226.

Ref: VALENCIENNES, 1/100.000. 30/11/18.

---

1. The Battalion will move to-morrow, 1st Dec. to BERMERAIN by march route & billet at that place on night 1/2nd.
   ROUTE :- BRIASTRE - SOLESMES - MAISON BLEUE.

2. (a) Starting Point will be the junction of the QUIEVY - VIESLY Roads in BETHENCOURT Square as under :-

H. Q. Coy.	....	07.58	hours
Band } No 1 Coy. }	....	07.59	"
4 "	....	08.01	"
3 "	....	08.02	"
2 "	....	08.03	"
Police, Pioneers, Aid-Post & H.Q.San. Squad.	.....	08.04	"
Transport	.....	08.05	"

   (b) 100 yds. distance will be observed between companies & between Battn. & transport.

3. DRESS.- Marching Order. Steel helmets will be carried on the pack; blankets and jerkins on train transport.

4. (a) Officers' kits & mess boxes will be loaded at the Q.M's stores at 07.00 hrs.

   (b) Blankets (rolled in bundles of 10) will be dumped at Q.M's stores by 07.15 hours.
   Each company will detail one man who is unable to march to act as loading party. These will travel on the lorries.

   (c) Lewis guns will be packed to-night.

5. Dinners will be cooked on the line of march & eaten on arrival at BERMERAIN.

6. Men excused marching by the M.O. will report to Q.M. at 07.30 hours.

7. Billets will be left scrupulously clean : a certificate to this effect will be forwarded to Battn. H.Q. by 07.45 hours.

-----oo0oo-----

Capt. & Adjutant,
13th R. Fus.

ISSUED at...16.30...hrs.

Copy No 1 to C.O.
2 No 1 Coy.
3 2 "
4 3 "
5 4 "
6 Battn. H.Q.
7 Q.M.
8 T.O.
9 R.S.M.
10 File ✓
11 & 12 War Diary.

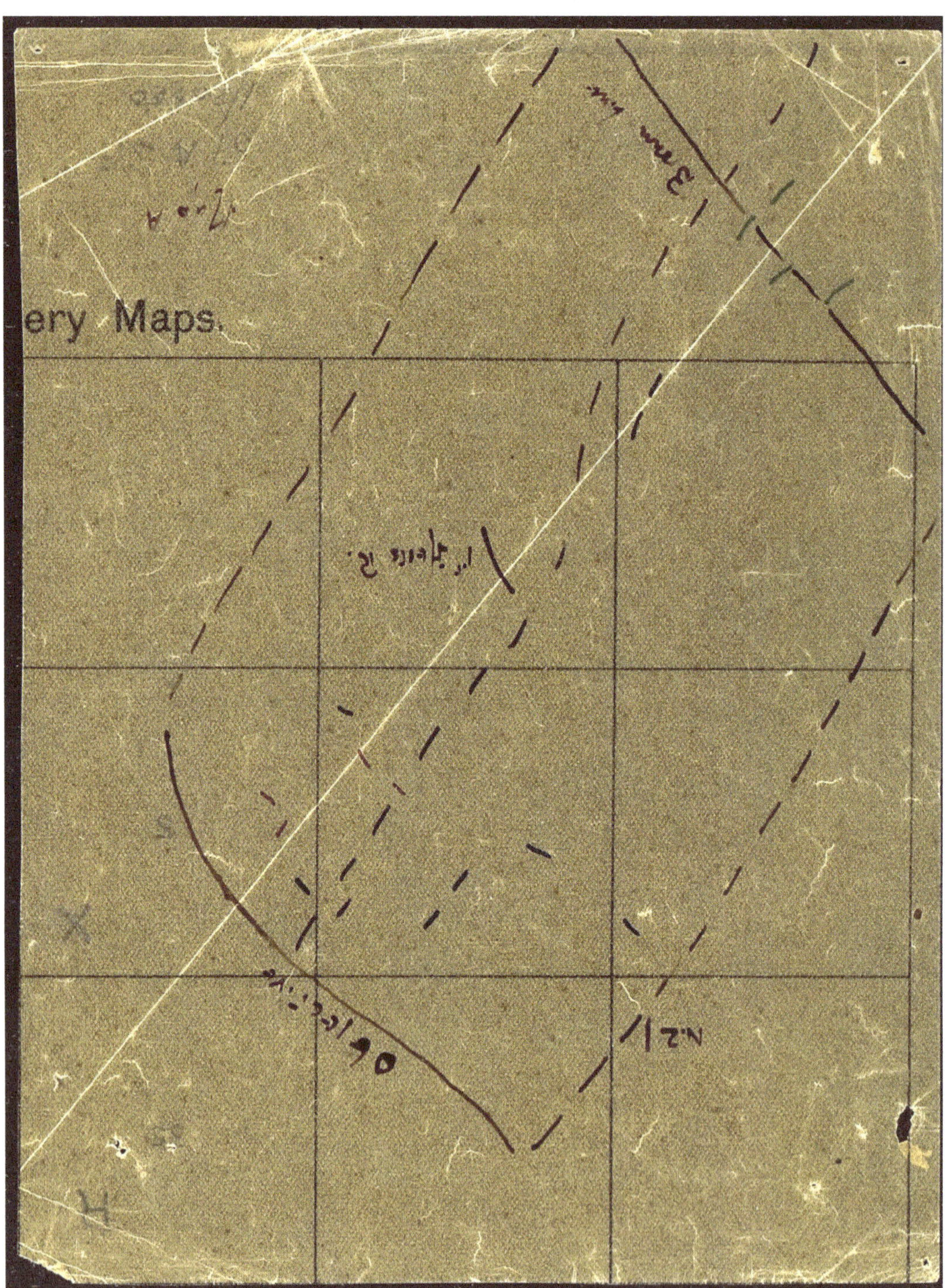
ery Maps.

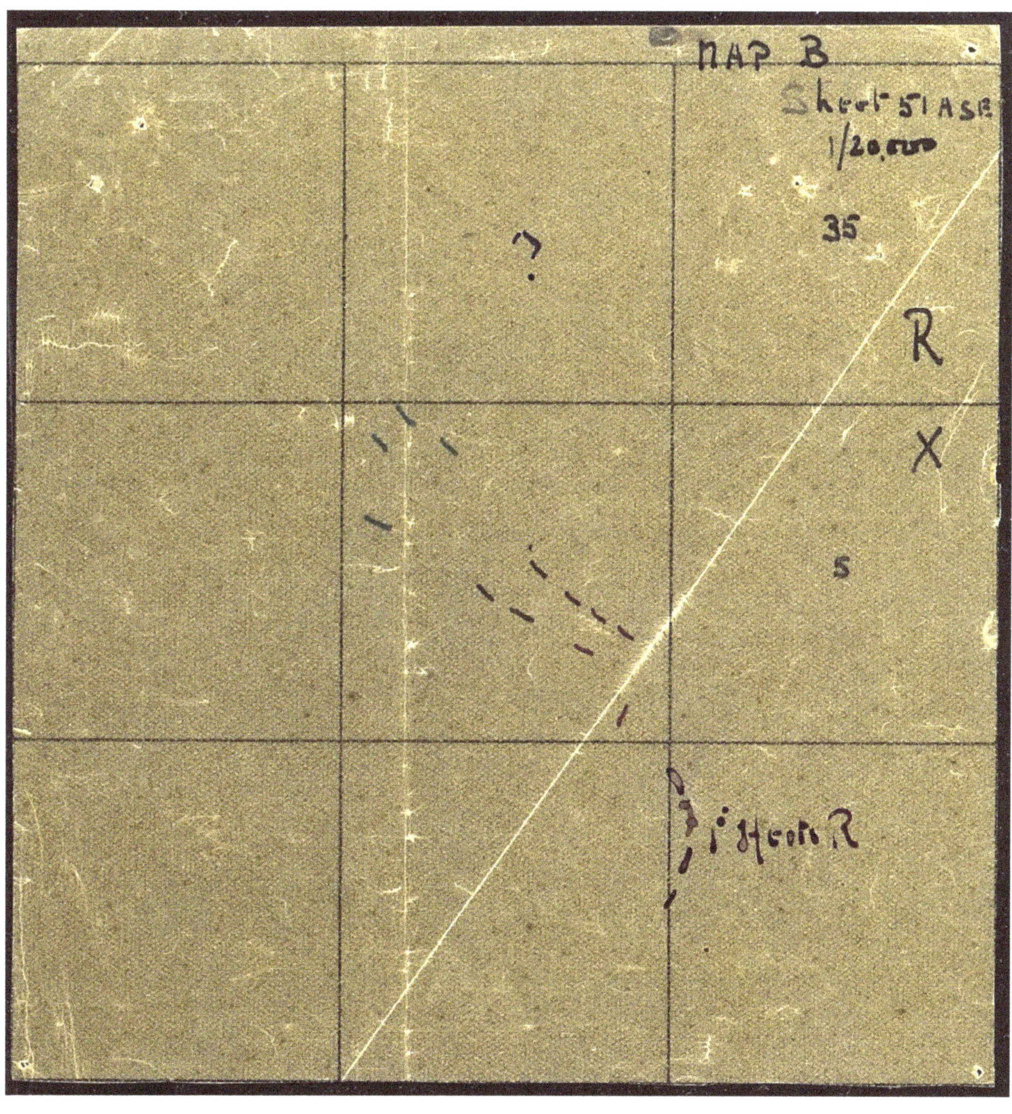
MAP B
Sheet 51 A SE
1/20,000
35
?
R
X
5

CONFIDENTIAL

WAR DIARY

OF

13TH BATTN.
ROYAL FUSILIERS

FOR THE MONTH OF

DECEMBER 1918

VOLUME 40

Instructions regarding War Diaries and Intelligence Summaries are contained in F. S. Regs., Part II. and the Staff Manual respectively. Title pages will be prepared in manuscript.

WAR DIARY
or
INTELLIGENCE SUMMARY.
(Erase heading not required.)

Army Form C. 2118.

Place	Date	Hour	Summary of Events and Information	Remarks and references to Appendices
	1/12/19		Strength of Battalion 36 Officers 723 Other Ranks.	
BETHENCOURT	"		Battalion moved by march route to BERMERAIN (VALENCIENNES, 1/100,000 3.G.) Order No. 227 issued.	APP. 111
BERMERAIN	2/12/19		Battalion moved by march route to WARGNIES-LE-GRAND (VALENCIENNES, 1/100,000 3.H.)	
WARGNIES-LE-GRAND	8/12/19		Lieut-Col. R.A. Smith, D.S.O.,M.C. resumed command of the Battalion.	
	[illegible]/12/19		Capt. J.K. Gwinnell rejoined battalion.	
	[illegible]/12/19		Training.	
	13/12/19		Order No. 228 issued.	
	14/12/19		Battalion moved to BELLIGNIES. Order No. 229 issued.	APP. 112 / 113
BELLIGNIES	15/12/19		Battalion moved to LA LONGUEVILLE (between BAVAI & MAUBEUGE)	
LA LONGUEVILLE	16/12/19		Battalion rested 24 hours. Order No. 230 issued.	114
	"		The following decorations were awarded :-	

THE MILITARY CROSS

Capt. G.G. Ziegler, . .
Lieut (Act.Capt) M.C. Lewis, .
2nd Lieut. A.H. Taylor

THE DISTINGUISHED CONDUCT MEDAL

No.61684 Sgt. E.J. Buckley No 3 Coy.
75213 Pte F.G. St.Pier 1 "
50970 " J. Wareham,M.M. 4 "

For conspicuous galantry & devotion to duty at GHISSIGNIES 24/10/18 (Authy :- 3rd Army R.O. d/- 3/12/18)

(A7092). Wt. W12839/M1293. 750,000. 1/17. D. D. & L., Ltd. Forms/C.2118/14.

Instructions regarding War Diaries and Intelligence Summaries are contained in F. S. Regs., Part II. and the Staff Manual respectively. Title pages will be prepared in manuscript.

WAR DIARY
or
INTELLIGENCE SUMMARY.
(Erase heading not required.)

Army Form C. 2118.

Place	Date	Hour	Summary of Events and Information	Remarks and references to Appendices
	14/12/18		The Military Medal was also awarded to Mlle. Marguerite LESNE who rendered considerable assistance to the wounded of the Battalion at GHISSIGNIES during the action on 24/10/18. This lady assisted wounded in the open under artillery fire.	
	17/12/18		Battalion moved to FAUBOURG DE MONS (N. of MAUBEUGE). Order No. 231 issued.	App 115
	18/12/18		Battalion moved to BINCHE. Bad weather. Order No. 232 issued.	116
BINCHE	19/12/18		Battalion moved to SOUVRET. Order No. 233 issued.	117
SOUVRET	20/12/18		Battalion moved to RANSART (N.E. of CHARLEROI). The leading Battalion of the Brigade missed the road. Battn. moved via MARCHIENNE & CHARLEROI. It rained.	
RANSART	21/12/18		Battn. settled in parmanent billets.	
	27/12/18		Battalion awarded the G.O.C. 37th Division silver cup for the best battalion on the march between 13 - 20th December.	
	28/12/18		Following mentioned in despatches (London Gazette 27/12/18) :- Lieut-Col. R.A.Smith,D.S.O.,M.C. Major T.J.E. Blake,D.S.O. Capt. (A/Major) T. H.Whitehead,D.S.O.,M.C. Capt. G.P. Chapman, Capt. J.K. Gwinnel, Capt. G.G, Ziegler,M.C. Lieut. H.Kirk,D.C.M. 2nd Lt. H.J. Keeble, P.S. 4789 Sgt. H. Etchells.	
	22-31/12/18		Training.	
			Strength of Battalion.- 40 Officers 703 Other Ranks.	

[signature] Capt. & Adjt. 13 R.F.

2353 Wt. W2544/1454 700,000 5/15 D. D. & L. A.D.S.S. Forms/C 2118.

13TH BN. RYL. FUSILIERS

War Diary.

VOLUME XLIII

JANUARY, 1919.

App 118

13th S. Battalion Royal Fusiliers

				Off.	O.R.
Strength of unit 1st January 1919.				40.	692
	Off.	O.R.			
(a) Increase during month.	-	25.			

	Off.	O.R.
(b) Decrease during month.		
Coalminers..................................	-	3.
Pivotals	-	11.
Long Service	-	20.
Watford Details	-	4.
Detained in England for demobilization	2	11.
Guarantee letter men, Serving Soldiers Releaseable Groups etc.	9	119.
(c) Evacuated sick..............................		7
(d) Other causes	1	2.
Total Decrease	12.	177.
" Increase	-	25.
Nett Decrease	12	152.

	Off.	O.R.
Nett Decrease	12.	152.
Strength of Unit January 31st. 1919.	28	540.

[signature] Capt. Adj. 13 R.F.

Instructions regarding War Diaries and Intelligence Summaries are contained in F. S. Regs., Part II. and the Staff Manual respectively. Title pages will be prepared in manuscript.

WAR DIARY
or
INTELLIGENCE SUMMARY.

(*Erase heading not required.*)

Army Form C. 2118.

Place	Date	Hour	Summary of Events and Information	Remarks and references to Appendices
RANSART (NAMUR 8 I F)	1919 Jan.		Strength of Battalion 40 Officers 692 Other Ranks.	
			Battalion in billets 3 miles N.N.E. of CHARLEROI.	
			<u>Training</u> : Practically no military training has been carried out. During week 21 - 27th Battn. was wholly employed as guards on dump at LODELINSART, MOTTE, DAMPREMY, RANSART.	
			<u>Education</u> : Classes have fallen off considerably. Knowledge for its own sake does not appeal to the average man. There is also a considerable dearth of trained instructors.	
			<u>Demobilization</u> : Five allotments have been received. For number of men demobilized see App.118. Great difficulty has been experienced in keeping up the necessary staff of the Battalion.- transport men, cooks, signallers, clerks, etc. There is a certain amount of very natural discontent, chiefly arising out of the mistakes of the Home Labour Ministry.	App. 119.
			No drafts have been received except men returned from hospital.	
			<u>Supplies</u> : All supplies have been bad. Mails are very irregular. Canteen supplies at a minimum.	
			<u>Divisional Commander's Cup</u> : The cup offered by G.O.C., 37th Division, for the best Battn. in the Division on the six day's march from the LE QUESNOY area to the GOSSELIES area has been won by the 13th Bn. Royal Fusiliers.	
			[signature] Capt. & Adj. 13 RF	

D. D. & L., London, E.C. (A8004) Wt. W1771/M2 31 750,000 5/17 Sch. 52 Forms/C2118/14

Army Form C. 2118.

WAR DIARY
or
INTELLIGENCE SUMMARY.

(Erase heading not required.)

Instructions regarding War Diaries and Intelligence Summaries are contained in F. S. Regs., Part II. and the Staff Manual respectively. Title pages will be prepared in manuscript.

Place	Date	Hour	Summary of Events and Information	Remarks and references to Appendices
			Honours & Rewards : The following decorations have been awarded during the month :-	

BAR TO MILITARY CROSS.
T/Lieut. (A/Capt.) H.W. Daniel, M.C.

BAR TO DISTINGUISHED CONDUCT MEDAL.
G5989 C.S.M. J.S. Edmonds, D.C.M., M.M.

DISTINGUISHED CONDUCT MEDAL.
2933 Sgt. T.G. Maloney.
71621 L/Cpl. R.V. Knights.

Action. HURTEBISE FARM (S. of LESDAIN) 8/10/18. Authy :- 3rd Army R.O. 1875 d/- 18.11.18.

MILITARY CROSS.
T/Capt. G.P. Chapman.

DISTINGUISHED CONDUCT MEDAL.
8021 Sgt. W. Green, M.M.

Action. FORET DE MORMAL 4/11/18. Authy :- 3rd Army R.O. d/- 18/12/18.

ORDER OF BRITISH EMPIRE.
T/Capt. G.P. Chapman, M.C. — London Gazette d/- 1/1/19.

MERITORIOUS SERVICE MEDAL.
No. L17086 R.S.M. R. Armour, M.C. — " 18/1/19.
G5936 C.Q.M.S. R.A. Thomerson. — " "

New Years Honours

Thanks of Town of CAUDRY : Letter from town of CAUDRY received 25th Oct. for action 10th Oct. 1918, should have been included in previous War Diary.

Strength of Battalion 29 Off. 540 O.Ranks.

App 119

G. P. Chapman, Capt. & Adjt. 13th R. Fus.

D. D. & L., London, E.C. (A8004) Wt. W1771/M2 31 750,000 5/17 Sch. 52 Forms/C2118/14

CONFIDENTIAL

WAR DIARY

OF

13TH Bn THE Ryl FUSILIERS

FOR THE MONTH OF

FEBRUARY 1919

VOLUME 45

Army Form C. 2118.

Instructions regarding War Diaries and Intelligence Summaries are contained in F. S. Regs., Part II. and the Staff Manual respectively. Title pages will be prepared in manuscript.

WAR DIARY
or
INTELLIGENCE SUMMARY.

(*Erase heading not required.*)

Place	Date	Hour	Summary of Events and Information	Remarks and references to Appendices
RANSART. (NAMUR 8. I. F.)	3/2/19.		Battalion remained in same billets.	
	"		The Kings Colour was presented to the Battalion, by Lieut. Gen. Sir G. HARPER, K.C.B. D.S.O. Commanding IV Corps.	
	7/2/19		Presentation of Medal Ribbons to Battalion by Maj-Gen. H.B. Williams, C.B. D.S.O. Commanding 37th. Division.	
	"		Orders received for draft of 10 Officers and 200 Other ranks to be sent to 17th. Bn. Royal Fusiliers. 5th. Brigade. 2nd. Division on 12th. inst.,	
	10/2/19		Date of move of draft cancelled.	
	16/2/19		Presentation by Maj-Gen. H.B. Williams C.B. D.S.O. of Cup to the Battalion, for the best Battalion in the Division on the march into Belgium	
	18/2/19		Part of Ordnance stores handed in.	
	26/2/19		Sale of "Z" horses commenced.	
	27/2/19		All "Y" horses sent to England.	

Lieut. & Adjutant.
13th. (S) BN. ROYAL FUSILIERS.

D. D. & L., London, E.C.
(A8004) Wt. W1771/M2 31 750,000 5/17 Sch. 52 Forms/C2118/14

Army Form C. 2118.

Instructions regarding War Diaries and Intelligence Summaries are contained in F. S. Regs., Part II. and the Staff Manual respectively. Title Pages will be prepared in manuscript.

WAR DIARY
or
INTELLIGENCE SUMMARY
(Erase heading not required.)

Vol 42

Place	Date MARCH	Hour 1919.	Summary of Events and Information	Remarks and references to Appendices
RANSART. Ref. Map NAMUR 8.	1st. "		Battalion in billets at RANSART. Draft of 8 Officers and 183 O. R's. proceeded to join the 17th. Bn. Royal Fusiliers.	
	2nd.		52 O. R's. left Battalion for demobilisation.	
	(3rd. (to (8th.		Without incident. Regimental duties.	
	9th. 10th.		Brigade Order No. AI30/1245 received to move to JUMET area. Battalion move to JUMET.	
	(11th. (to (31st.		Without incident. Regimental duties.	

	Off.	O. R's.
STRENGTH FOR 1/3/19	21	353
Decrease for month	14	290
	7	63
Increase for month	1	20
Strength for month ending 31st. March 1919.	8	83

[signature]
Lieut. & Adjutant.
13th. Bn. Royal Fusiliers.

2449 Wt. W14957/M90 750,000 1/16 J.B.C. & A. Forms/C.2118/12.

40.P

Effective Strength for February Ist 1919.	Offs	O.R.
	28	537

Lieut S.M. Adler to England sick
Lieut E.S. Hart M.C. retained in England pending Demob.
2nd. Lt A.H. Starling Demobilized
" " C.W. Randall -do-
" " H.B. Wolfestan -do-
" " J.B. Medgshon -do-
" " G.S. Gibbons -do-

Demobilized	160	O.Ranks
Ret. in Eng. pending Demob.	6	"
Evac. sick	13	
Trans. to 2nd. Army H.Q.	1	
To Hosp. whilst on leave	1	
	181	

	Offs.	O.Ranks
Strength for February Ist 1919	28	537
Decrease for month	7	181
Strength for end of month	21	356

H J Ruth Lt

March 1919

Lieut & Adjutant
for C.C. 13th Bn. Royal Fusiliers

Translation of a letter from the Maire of Caudry.

The Mayor of CAUDRY,

to the G.O.C. French Mission attached to British Armies.

General,

I beg to convey to the Colonel commanding the 13th Royal Fusiliers the warmest thanks, both of the Municipality and of the population, on the conspicuous gallantry of the troops that have taken a part in the capture of Caudry.

Personally, I make it a point to express my gratitude to the Officers, N.C.O's and men of the 13th Royal Fusiliers for the glorious achievement they have atteined in driving the enemy from Caudry.

The warm and enthusiastic reception with which the population has greeted the British troops, our liberators, clearly shows that four years of oppression have not abated the patriotic spirit of our people.

Now can I end this letter without pointing out the high services rendered to the above population by the members of the French Mission. All of them, irrespective of rank, have much contributed to establishing a friendly intercourse between the Civilians and the British Authorities.

With renewed thanks, believe me, General

etc......etc.-

Checked

To be corrected

Legend.

13th R.Fus.

No 4 Coy	——
" 1 "	——
" 2 "	——
" 3 "	——
1/1st Herts } [illegible] 2 Div }	——

www.ingramcontent.com/pod-product-compliance
Lightning Source LLC
Chambersburg PA
CBHW081548160426
43191CB00011B/1870

9781474518338